As one of the world's longest established
and best-known travel brands,
Thomas Cook are the experts in travel.

For more than 135 years our
guidebooks have unlocked the secrets
of destinations around the world,
sharing with travellers a wealth of
experience and a passion for travel.

**Rely on Thomas Cook as your
travelling companion on your next trip
and benefit from our unique heritage.**

Thomas Cook **traveller** guides

PARIS

ELISABETH MORRIS

Thomas
Cook

Your travelling companion since 1873

Written by Elisabeth Morris, updated by Petulia Melideo
Original photography by Anthony Soutter and Ken Patterson

Published by Thomas Cook Publishing
A division of Thomas Cook Tour Operations Limited
Company registration no. 3772199 England
The Thomas Cook Business Park, Unit 9, Coningsby Road,
Peterborough PE3 8SB, United Kingdom
Email: books@thomascook.com, Tel: +44 (0) 1733 416477
www.thomascookpublishing.com

Produced by Cambridge Publishing Management Limited
Burr Elm Court, Main Street, Caldecote CB23 7NU
www.cambridgepm.co.uk

ISBN: 978-1-84848-477-1

© 2002, 2005, 2007, 2009 Thomas Cook Publishing
This fifth edition © 2011
Text © Thomas Cook Publishing
Maps © Thomas Cook Publishing/PCGraphics (UK) Limited
Transport map © Communicarta Limited

Series Editor: Karen Beaulah
Production/DTP: Steven Collins

Printed and bound in Spain by GraphyCems

Cover photography © Sylvain Sonnet

Contents

Introduction

Fluctuat nec mergitur ('she is buffeted by the waves but she does not sink') has been the city's proud motto for more than four centuries ... and still holds true today. Through revolutions, wars, foreign occupation and, above all, redevelopment, Paris has remained true to her image for generation after generation of enthusiastic admirers.

The sheer beauty of the capital conquers first-time visitors. A harmonious ensemble of splendid monuments and elegant domestic architecture provides a unique impression of unity; moreover, everything seems to be in its rightful place, from the Madeleine matching the Assemblée Nationale across place de la Concorde to the unobtrusive place Dauphine at the tip of Île de la Cité. Yet subtle planning and inspired improvisation are constantly remodelling the seemingly perfect image of Paris, and while pessimists predict that 'it will never be the same again', these innovations are being enthusiastically accepted by Parisians and outsiders alike. To give a few examples: the Eiffel Tower, which raised such an outcry when it was built more than a hundred years ago, has become the most familiar landmark of the city; the controversial Centre Pompidou is now the most visited monument; and the Louvre would already seem incomplete without its pyramid.

Recent changes in the Parisian cultural panorama include the Musée du quai Branly, a modern structure set

FAMOUS PARISIANS

Plaques on buildings throughout the city commemorate famous Parisians.

Parisians by birth:
- **Molière**, playwright at the court of Louis XIV.
- **George Sand**, romantic novelist.
- The sculptor **Auguste Rodin**, whose house is now a museum.
- The Montmartre painter **Maurice Utrillo**.
- Existentialist philosopher **Jean-Paul Sartre**.
- Cabaret singer **Maurice Chevalier**.

Parisians by adoption:
- The painters **Eugène Delacroix** and **Vincent van Gogh**.
- Legendary composer **Frédéric Chopin**.
- Author and playwright **Oscar Wilde**, who ended his life in St-Germain-des-Prés.
- **Ernest Hemingway**, who lived in Paris during the 1920s and '30s.
- Cubist **Pablo Picasso**.
- **The Duke and Duchess of Windsor**, who lived in the exclusive avenue Foch.

in the traditional and residential neighbourhood of the 10th *arrondissement*. This museum, entirely dedicated to cultures from Africa, Asia, Oceania and the Americas, created a stir when it opened, while now it represents one of the must-sees on the list of every visitor coming to Paris.

However, beauty alone does not explain the attraction of Paris for so many. One could argue in favour of its vast cultural wealth, its *haute couture,* or its reputation in the field of entertainment. Along with art and fashion, Paris is regaining its crown as culinary capital of the world. After a few years of sleepy traditional French food, the City of Light is moving at a quick pace in the race for innovative restaurants, artisanal cuisine and better customer service. However, its magical appeal is due mainly to an undefinable charm that seems to spring quite unexpectedly from the many facets of everyday life. Ordinary details, no matter how trivial, suddenly seem to acquire a new dimension: it could be a quaint-looking kiosk on a street corner; a white-globed street lamp in the middle of a tiny square; an old-fashioned shopfront; the *bouquinistes* (second-hand bookstalls) in the morning mist; or just an evocative street name such as the rue du Chat-qui-Pêche (fishing cat street).

Full of contradictions, Paris never ceases to surprise: at once compact and spacious, it can be in turn pompous and modest, cheap and outrageously expensive, enthralling and infuriating, depending on the place and time of day.

A typically Parisian fusing of contemporary and classical styles

History

52 BC	Romans conquer the island; the settlement prospers and spreads to the left bank.
c. AD 280	Barbarians raid city. The Parisii flee to the island.
c.360	Paris gets its name.
451	Attila's Huns attack. The young Geneviève predicts the town will be spared; she is later made the city's patron saint.
508	The first Christian king of the Franks, Clovis, makes Paris his capital.
1163	Notre-Dame Cathedral is begun by Maurice de Sully, Bishop of Paris.
1180	King Philippe-Auguste orders a new city wall and the Louvre fortress.
1215	The first university in France is founded in Paris.
1253	The Sorbonne is founded.
1364	Charles V starts to build a new wall around Paris and the Bastille.
1420	Height of the Hundred Years War: the English occupy Paris.
1430	Henry VI of England crowned king of France.
1436	Charles VII recaptures the city.
1546	New Renaissance palace at the Louvre begun.
1572	Saint Bartholomew's Day massacre. Several thousand Huguenots die.
1578–1604	The Pont Neuf is built.
Late 17th century	Louis XIV moves to Versailles, founds the Invalides.
c.1760	Louis XV commissions the École Militaire, the Panthéon and place de la Concorde.
1789	The fall of the Bastille (14 July): beginning of the French Revolution.
1792	Proclamation of the First Republic.
1793	Louis XVI guillotined.

1804	Napoleon is crowned emperor in Notre-Dame.
Early 19th century	Arc de Triomphe is built.
1848	Louis-Napoleon elected first president of the Second Republic.
1852–70	Baron Haussmann remodels Paris.
1870–71	Third Republic is proclaimed. The Paris Commune is crushed.
1889	Tour Eiffel built for the Exposition Universelle.
1900	First métro line opened. Montmartre witnesses the birth of modern art.
1914	Paris is saved from German invasion by the Battle of the Marne.
1937	The Palais de Chaillot and the Palais de Tokyo built for the Exposition Universelle.
1940	Paris bombed and occupied by the Germans.
1944	Paris is liberated.
1958	Work starts on La Défense.
1977	Paris' first mayor since 1871 is elected and the Centre Pompidou is opened.
1986	Musée d'Orsay and the Cité des Sciences are inaugurated.
1996	Mitterrand officially opens the Bibliothèque Nationale de France.
2002	Euro notes and coins enter circulation.
2004	Centenary of the *Entente Cordiale* between Britain and France.
2007	France hosts the Rugby World Cup.
2008	Nicolas Sarkozy elected president of France.
2009	International Year of Astronomy launched at UNESCO headquarters in Paris.
2010	Under President Sarkozy the French senate votes overwhelmingly to ban the wearing of face-covering veils in public.
2012	Disneyland® Paris celebrates its 20th anniversary.

The city

Paris is situated in northern France, at the centre of a vast natural chalk basin drained by the River Seine and its numerous tributaries, including the Marne and the Oise.

Île-de-France

The area surrounding Paris is, as its name suggests, the very heart of France. This privilege goes back to the 6th century, when the region already formed the core of the kingdom of the Franks. Rich agricultural land, green valleys, beautiful forests, a temperate climate, easy communications and the presence of the capital in its centre secured its supremacy over the rest of the country.

However, the division of the whole French territory into some 90 *départements* at the end of the 18th century made the region's limits rather difficult to define. It was, for a long time, vaguely referred to as the 'Paris Region' and the name Île-de-France seemed to be relegated to history books.

In 1976 France was divided into 22 regions, each including several *départements,* and Paris Region was officially given back its original name of Île-de-France. The region comprises Paris and seven other *départements* clustering round the capital.

Since the introduction of gradual decentralisation over the past 20 years, the region has been governed by a *Conseil Régional* consisting of 197 councillors elected for a period of six years, assisted by a *Comité Économique et Social*, which advises on specific projects.

THE TRUE PARISIAN

The population of Paris, like that of many large towns, has, with the influx of immigrants, become so cosmopolitan that the notion of a 'true Parisian' may seem like a myth. But visitors need have no fear: the true Parisian is still very real.

He or she may have come originally from a different part of France, or even from abroad, but once adopted by Paris becomes a true Parisian: hurrying along the pavements and the métro corridors, hurrying to work and hurrying back home again in the evening, hurrying through life, in fact . . . not particularly amiable, especially if at the wheel of a car, but quick-witted and able to enjoy life intensely for a fleeting moment.

Nothing shocks or even surprises Parisians, and they would even be very tolerant ... if there were time!

Economy

Île-de-France is an area of great economic wealth, modelled by its illustrious past but definitely looking to the future. It covers only 2.2 per cent of France, but accommodates a fifth of the population and has no fewer than five 'new towns'. It is by far the most densely populated of all the regions, and contributes more than a quarter of the gross national product. Commerce, transport and service industries are well developed, accounting for nearly three-quarters of jobs. The industrial sector is almost as strong and produces a quarter of France's industrial wealth. Power generation, electronics, publishing and printing, pharmaceutical products, environmental technology, information and communications technology, as well as food, are the main industries.

Agriculture, on the other hand, although far from negligible and highly efficient, is economically very much in the background and specialises more and more in the intensive production of cereals, flowers and ornamental plants.

The city

Dominated by the Seine and neatly enclosed within a mostly efficient ring road (the Périphérique which can be very frustrating during the rush hour), Paris covers an area of a mere 105sq km (40½sq miles) divided into 20 *arrondissements*.

The population of the capital has now stabilised at just over 2 million inhabitants. During the past 15 years the tendency has been for people to move out of Paris and settle in other *départements* of the region, which Parisians call *la banlieue* (the suburbs). The areas surrounding the capital are officially referred to as *la petite couronne* (the close suburbs) and *la grande couronne* (the outskirts).

One of Notre-Dame's rooftop creatures enjoys the best view in the city

Politics

Paris owes its unique economic and cultural drive to its long-standing role as capital of France. It took an active part in all the major events of French history, suffering greatly during the more sombre periods of revolution and war, but always recovering and regaining its vitality, wit and artistic taste.

The corridors of power

Today there are in France three distinct components of government: the parliament, the government and the president.

Parliament consists of two houses: the Assemblée Nationale, elected for five years, sits in Palais Bourbon facing place de la Concorde and it discusses and votes on the laws; the Sénat, elected for nine years and housed in Palais du Luxembourg, has a purely advisory role.

The government is made up of the prime minister, chosen by the president, and a variable number of ministers. Together they are answerable to the Assemblée Nationale for their policies. The prime minister resides in Hôtel Matignon, in Faubourg St-Germain.

The président de la République is elected for five years; he (so far, they have all been men) chooses the prime minister and presides over cabinet meetings. He is head of the armed forces, has considerable powers in foreign affairs, ensures the independence of the judiciary and may be granted special powers in exceptional circumstances. Palais de l'Élysée is his official residence.

Helping to turn the wheels of power, the political parties and trade unions are all based in the capital, as are the national newspapers.

Finally one must not forget the people of Paris, who have always shown great interest in the running of national affairs and who take an active part in decision-making through frequent street demonstrations and gatherings in public squares.

Embassies from countries all over the world have long been established in the capital, which is also the seat of major international organisations such as UNESCO (United Nations Educational, Scientific and Cultural Organization) and OECD (Organisation for Economic Cooperation and Development).

Paris has lately become the most sought-after centre of international congress in the world, overtaking London and Brussels.

The changing face of Paris

The endowment on the local authority of real powers proved beneficial to the city as it enabled the municipality and the state to share the responsibility for the capital's great architectural heritage and to initiate daring futuristic projects aimed at maintaining Paris's position as one of the major modern European cities. Even if everything has not always gone smoothly, the results so far are stunning: whole districts that had become derelict have been restored (such as the Marais), or completely rebuilt (such as the Halles or Paris Rive Gauche), but their traditions have been preserved. At the same time, the renovation of eastern districts, neglected for far too long, was inspired by bold town-planning principles with astonishing results: thus La Villette, in the northeast, is now a major cultural attraction.

Excitement over the changing face of Paris is not about to abate, especially since communications and the environment have become very controversial issues in local politics.

France is in a period of flux. The country has the highest degree of productivity in Europe: the French work very hard, but in return they enjoy lengthy holidays. A large percentage of the French population realises that change to the social system is necessary; many are also very reluctant to give up their benefits.

President Sarkozy has been, more than anyone before, a president under the glare of the media. At first it was his wealthy origins and his entrepreneurial approach to politics that caught media attention – as the 23rd French president, one of his first actions was to give himself a pay rise. Later, it became his personal life – the divorce from his first wife Cécilia Ciganer-Albéniz and the subsequent marriage to top model Carla Bruni.

Politics

Palais de Justice – its beauty belies its turbulent history

Culture

Foreigners usually expect to discover in Paris the very essence of French culture, and they are right to a certain extent, although provincial French people would not agree, however proud they may be of their capital. Wit, elegance and energy are all to be found in Paris. Parisians are aware that the rest of France is watching them and have always been keen to rise to the challenge. As a result, they have developed a strong need to innovate, as well as a tremendous drive to achieve their goals.

Despite its rich heritage and great monuments, Paris is still experimenting with new architecture. The city is reclaiming abandoned factories and disused railroad tracks around the Périphérique ('beltway') to create a whole neighbourhood, such as the 'new' Rive Gauche that now surrounds the four towers of the Bibliothèque Nationale de France (completed in 1996). In the surrounding streets there are art galleries (rue Louis Weiss has seven), cafés, restaurants and boutiques, as well as the University of Paris 7. As part of that project the 1921 building that housed the Grands Moulins, or flour mills, has become the university library.

A certain way of life

Parisians may be fond of new ideas but they are also conservative, and their lifestyle reflects this constant conflict between innovation and tradition. Paris has always been a compact city and Parisians have become used to living in cramped conditions, in blocks of flats that traditionally have six storeys and a concierge (caretaker) on the ground floor. Therefore street life is important to them: local bistros, brasseries and cafés are a favourite meeting place throughout the day. Open-air markets, where people from different generations and social backgrounds mingle in a colourful display of exuberance, have remained the focal point of many districts.

Furthermore, Parisians have a reputation for trendsetting: a district suddenly becomes fashionable and everyone wants to live in it. This phenomenon is also apparent in two other important aspects of Parisian life – clothing and food, where there is a definite cosmopolitan influence.

Subtle changes

The traditional way of life is gradually changing as the fabric of the population itself alters: the number of workers in high-tech industries, members of the professional classes, and artists is increasing rapidly, while the contrast between wealthy western districts and poorer eastern areas is disappearing. At the same time the pace of living has quickened considerably, inevitably damaging personal contacts. On the other hand Paris is becoming truly cosmopolitan, which has brought greater cultural variety to the Parisian scene.

Culture for everyone

Paris is, as much as ever, a melting pot of artistic creation and a place where one can never tire of being a spectator. Music, drama and the visual arts are taught at various levels, from the municipal schools to the national *conservatoires.*

Paris is also the place to visit for those who do not take an active part in culture but thrive on it. There are, of course, prestigious opera houses, concert halls and theatres, but there are also free concerts in many churches all over the city, and avant-garde plays in tiny, obscure theatres.

In addition to their permanent collections, museums and art galleries organise temporary exhibitions. The number of libraries is increasing rapidly, and there is still a record number of cinemas in spite of fierce competition from television. Also, this brief review of the cultural scene would be incomplete without a special mention of two great multipurpose cultural centres: the Centre Pompidou, and the music and science complex at La Villette.

The stately 16th-century Louvre, now served by its glass-pyramid information centre

Festivals and events

Festivals stem from an ancient tradition, but their number has greatly increased in recent years and they have developed from spontaneous, regular gatherings into elaborate forms of entertainment aimed at occasional visitors as well as local residents. Below are some of the regular highlights.

In Paris

Festival 'Foire St-Germain'
Jun–Jul
Theatre, music, exhibitions and an antiques fair in St-Germain-des-Prés.
Tel: 01 43 29 61 04.

Paris Jazz Festival *Jun–Aug*
Parc Floral de Paris.
www.parisjazzfestival.fr

Festival Chopin *mid-Jun–mid-Jul*
Concerts and recitals in the Parc de Bagatelle.
Tel: 01 45 00 22 19.
www.frederic-chopin.com

Paris Plage *mid-Jul–mid-Aug*
The Right Bank from pont Henri IV to quai des Tuileries is transformed into mini-beaches. *www.paris-plages.fr*

Festival Musique en l'Île *Jul–Sept*
Classical music in Église St-Louis-en-L'Île. *Tel: 01 55 42 81 33.*
www.eglise-sgp.org

La Villette Jazz Festival *Sept*
Grand Hall, La Villette.
Tel: 01 44 84 44 84/01 40 03 75 75.

Journée du Patrimoine *Sept*
A countrywide event where normally off-limits buildings such as the Palais d'Élysée are opened to the public.
www.journeesdupatrimoine.culture.fr

Festival d'Automne *mid-Sept–end Dec*
Music, dance, plays and special exhibitions. *Tel: 01 53 45 17 17.*
www.festival-automne.com

La Nuit Blanche *first Sat night in Oct*
Museums, shops and monuments are open and free during the night. Lots of special events, parties and performances.
http://nuitblanche.paris.fr

FIAC *end of Oct*
Four days of contemporary art displayed across various locations including the Grand Palais.
Tel: 01 47 56 64 21. www.fiac.com

In Île-de-France
Rueil-Malmaison *Jan*
Festival International du Film
d'Histoire, devoted to
historical films.
Tel: 01 47 14 54 54.
www.mediatheque-rueilmalmaison.fr

Versailles *Apr–Oct*
Enjoy the gardens of Versailles
at their best, to a backdrop of
Baroque music and the splash
of fountains.
www.chateauversailles.fr

Abbaye de Royaumont
May, Jun, Sept & Oct
Concerts take place in abbey
buildings.
www.royaumont.com

Fontainebleau *Jul & Aug*
Concerts are given in the castle.
www.musee-chateau-fontainebleau.fr

St-Germain-en-Laye *Sept*
International music festival featuring
works by the composer Claude
Debussy.

Suresnes *1st weekend Oct*
8km (5 miles) west of Paris, a wine
festival celebrates the harvests.
www.suresnes.fr

Fairs and special events
Foire du Trône *Mar–May*
A funfair in the Bois de Vincennes.
www.foiredutrone.com

Fête de la Musique *21 Jun*
In the 20 *arrondissements* of Paris.
Tel: 01 40 03 94 70.
www.fetedelamusique.culture.fr

La Fête Nationale *13–14 Jul*
A huge open-air ball on the place de la
Bastille, followed by a military parade
along the Champs-Élysées on the
morning of 14 July and fireworks in the
evening at the Trocadéro.

Fête des Tuileries *Jul–mid-Aug & Dec*
Funfair in the Jardin des Tuileries.
Métro: Tuileries.

Art exhibitions
Salon des Artistes Indépendants *Apr*
Art exhibitions with different themes.
*L'Espace Champerret, Porte de
Champerret, 75017. Métro: Porte de
Charenton or Balard/Créteil.*

**Les Cinq Jours de l'Objet
Extraordinaire** *late May*
A display of antiques by dealers of
the Carré Rive Gauche, 75007.

**Foire Internationale d'Art
Contemporain** *end Oct*
Contemporary art at the Grand Palais,
Cour Carrée du Louvre and Jardin
des Tuileries. *www.fiac.com.*
Métro: Louvre-Rivoli.

Salon d'Automne *Nov*
Paintings, sculptures, photographs and
architecture. *L'Espace Charenton, 327
rue de Charenton, 75012.*

Impressions

Whether you are there only for a weekend or you are able to enjoy a longer stay, Paris will not disappoint. A true European capital, the City of Lights shines for the variety of its museums, the abundance of its shops, the beauty of its boulevards and parks and of course its delicious cuisine to be found in the restaurants scattered throughout its timeless streets.

When to go

In summer Paris belongs to the tourists. If you are looking for authenticity August is the worst month to visit, as the city is deserted by Parisians, cultural activities are at a low ebb, many restaurants and shops are closed and the weather can be uncomfortably humid.

Winter has a certain charm, with statues and monuments looking stark through the leafless trees, but the days are short. Crowds in the streets reach their peak at Christmas time, a particularly lively period. January, with its traditional sales, is a good time for shopping.

However, late spring and early autumn are the most exciting seasons in which to visit Paris: in spring, parks and gardens are a haven of freshness, while the long warm evenings invite you to stroll along the Seine or watch the sun set, the Arc de Triomphe ablaze. There is a holiday spirit in the air that brings smiles and humour into everyday conversation.

Autumn marks the start of the return to the city – *la rentrée*, as the French call it. Restaurants, theatres and opera houses reopen, major exhibitions are announced, new trends in fashion are set and children go back to school; moreover, Parisians are at their

THOMAS COOK'S PARIS

Thomas Cook undertook his first-ever trip abroad to the Paris Exhibition in 1855. Because he couldn't get a concession on the Channel crossing he went from Harwich to Brussels, down the Rhine to Strasbourg and then overland to Paris. The party included four unaccompanied sisters who, although criticised for their daring, felt they could venture anywhere escorted by Mr Cook. (Cook's subsequent tours were heavily patronised by single women, whose travel horizons would otherwise have been limited by Victorian ideas of propriety.)

The total cost of the first trip, including expenses, was estimated by one of the sisters at £10. Paris became a favourite destination for Cook's parties, and his guidebook to Paris became a standard guide until the outbreak of World War II.

friendliest after their holidays spent away from the capital.

Getting around

On arrival you might take a taxi and be whirled round place Charles-de-Gaulle, which continues to be referred to as l'Étoile. This can be a hair-raising experience, but you will quickly come to terms with it when you realise that the *priorité à droite* (priority to vehicles coming from the right) really works – most of the time, anyway! From then on the pace is set, and you begin to get the feel of the place.

By car is definitely not the best way of exploring the French capital, both because of the large volume of traffic and the time restrictions on parking. Therefore, if you have travelled to France by car your best course of action is to leave it in a long-term car park (ask your hotel for information on the nearest one) and take to the streets.

Walking is by far the best way to visit the centre as distances are manageable and there are no hills. However, sooner or later you will need to use some form of public transport. Paris is a densely populated, compact city, but careful planning has provided it with wide avenues and two main thoroughfares along the Seine.

Finding your bearings

Paris is relatively small and some of the familiar landmarks act as beacons: the Sacré-Cœur Basilica on top of Montmartre is due north, the Eiffel Tower is to the west and the Montparnasse Tower dominates the southern part of town. Getting a detailed map should be your first move. All street signs show which *arrondissement* you are in, and if you look these up in the index of your Paris street plan it will even give you the nearest métro station.

An aerial view of the city

Areas of Paris

The areas situated on either side of the Seine have acquired their own character, but there is a distinction dear to the heart of Parisians between the right bank on the north side and the left bank in the south. It goes back to the Middle Ages, when the growing city started to spread along the banks of the river.

The left bank, or *rive gauche*, became the students' headquarters and has since been the favourite haunt of a lively bohemian society. The Quartier Latin, St-Germain-des-Prés and Montparnasse have all been favoured by intellectuals at different times. Meanwhile, the right bank, or *rive droite*, is traditionally conservative. A centre of business and commerce, it prides itself on having all the major department stores and *haute couture* boutiques (*see* Fashion, *pp148–9*).

Even Montmartre, at one time renowned as the poor artists' quarter, has acquired a definite respectability and been overrun by tourists, while the authenticity of the red-light district of Pigalle, at the bottom of the hill, has almost disappeared.

Over the years, however, the differences between left and right bank have, in other parts of the city, become more blurred. The area of the Marais, once a traditional Jewish neighbourhood, is now favoured by artsy, trendy Parisians who make this their favourite hang-out place. The Jewish institutions such as synagogues and kosher bakeries survive, now next door to gay bars and art galleries.

The left bank, traditionally a bohemian hang-out, is increasingly becoming a favourite destination for tourists, fashionistas and sophisticated art collectors. The areas around St Germain, rue de la Paix and rue Bonaparte are packed with expensive boutiques, tea rooms and beautiful restaurants.

As the population of Paris increases and more wealth flows into the city, the areas that were once considered no-gos gradually become trendy locations. A perfect example of this is the streets around Oberkampf and the Canal St Martin – a formerly frowned-upon neighbourhood that now attracts hordes of young couples and visitors.

Where to go

You might find the following suggestions helpful when choosing a walk or an area to visit.

If you like medieval architecture and enchanting river settings, go to Île de la Cité and Île St-Louis.

If you feel like taking it easy and mingling with a young crowd, aim for the Quartier Latin or St-Germain-des-Prés and watch the world go by from one of the lively cafés.

If you are feeling energetic enough to take on monumental Paris, walk up the Champs-Élysées or experience the thrill of admiring the city from the top of the Eiffel Tower.

If you enjoy shopping in a grand way, the Madeleine/Opéra area and the streets around St Germain are perfect. For more up-and-coming trends and smaller boutiques, the area around Bastille and the Marais is the most stimulating.

If discreet elegance appeals to you, and you enjoy taking in the art galleries, the Marais is where you want to be.

If you like modern architecture, take the métro to La Villette and the Paris Rive Gauche or the RER (*see p20*) to La Défense.

And if a desire for *la bohème* (bohemia) compels you to go to Montmartre, watch the artists at work on Place du Tertre and then pause to admire the view from Sacré-Cœur.

Coping with the weather

On a rainy day the main cultural centres such as La Villette (*see p103*) and the Centre Pompidou (*see p22*) offer varied activities for all ages, as well as meals and refreshments. Alternatively, the grand department stores on boulevard Haussmann are so

Paris's famous métro system makes getting around the city easy

close to one another that you can go from one to the other without getting wet. Or why not take the opportunity to discover one of the lovely old shopping arcades located near the Palais Royal, or stroll among the 250 boutiques of the Louvre des Antiquaires (*see p146*)?

Public transport

The métro, the RER and the buses are part of a very efficient system. The métro, short for *métropolitain*, is a mostly underground network of 15 lines covering the city within the Périphérique. Trains are frequent, stations are close to one another and there is one flat fare throughout. You can either buy tickets in batches of ten (*carnet*) or get a *Paris-Visite* pass for unlimited travel anywhere for a specified number of days; you can combine it with a *Carte Musée-Monuments* (museum pass).

Maps of the whole network are posted outside stations and on platforms. You can change from one line to another at intersection points by following the sign *correspondance*. The métro runs daily from 5.30am to 12.30am; buses from 6.30am to either 8.30pm or 12.30am. *Noctambus* (the night bus) operates on 18 routes between 1am and 5.35am (*see pp185–8* for more information on transport).

Travelling on the métro can be hectic, especially during the rush hour. A journey by bus is usually an enjoyable experience, but don't forget to allow

extra time and to ring the bell when you want to get off. The same tickets are used on buses as on the métro, but you may need two on the bus depending on the length of your journey.

Route finders, which look like cash dispensers, are called SITU. They are programmed to work out the quickest way to any destination by one or several means of transport, including walking.

The RER (Réseau Express Régional) is a suburban network of fast trains linked to the métro. The flat-fare system applies only within the city boundaries. The RER is a favoured means of transport between Orly and Charles de Gaulle airports and the centre of Paris.

Batobus Riverbuses operate (*Apr–Sept*) between the Eiffel Tower and the Hôtel de Ville, stopping at the main sights.

Taxis The best place to get one is from a *tête de station* (taxi rank) although you may have to wait for a while, especially on rainy days. Drivers accept a maximum of three or four passengers and expect a tip.

Velib In 2009 the city of Paris introduced a bike-sharing scheme called Velib. The bikes are located throughout the city, in visible dedicated areas. Short-term subscriptions (1 day or 1 week) are available to visitors. *www.velib.paris.fr*

Within the Périphérique

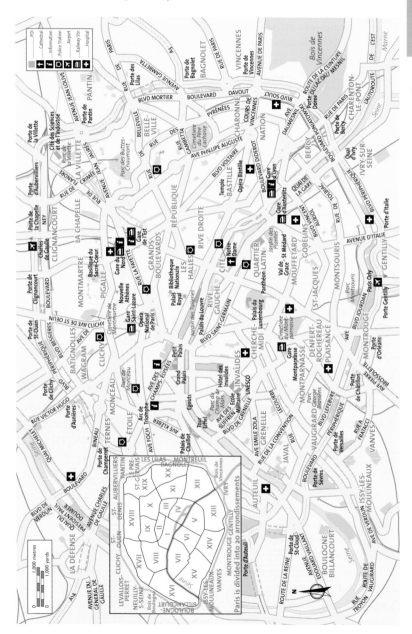

Paris is divided into 20 arrondissements

The historic centre

Packed with history and charm, the historic centre of Paris is the perfect place to start your visit. From the Île de la Cité, always busy with tourists, to the quiet and sophisticated Île St-Louis, and from the fashionable area around St-Germain-des-Prés to the busy hub of Les Halles, the historic centre of Paris offers something for everyone.

BEAUBOURG AND FORUM DES HALLES

This is very much an up-and-coming district, developing around the ultra-modern Forum des Halles and rapidly regaining the popularity it lost as a result of the departure of the colourful but obsolete food market that gave the area its name (*halle* means covered market).

Centre Georges Pompidou

The renovation occurred as a part of the huge town-planning programme centred around the Les Halles area during the 1970s. President Pompidou then decided to build a multi-purpose centre for modern and contemporary art on the site.

Its full name – **Centre National d'Art et de Culture Georges Pompidou** – gives a fair idea of the vast scope of this versatile cultural centre, and explains its enormous popularity, in spite of the controversy that still surrounds its design more than 30 years on.

Two young architects, Richard Rogers (British) and Renzo Piano (Italian), designed the complex, which was inaugurated in 1977, three years after President Pompidou's death. To some people it looks like an oil refinery or even scaffolding on a building site, while others, with a more optimistic outlook, see it as a contemporary piece of sculpture. In order to have as much free space as possible inside, lifts, stairs, escalators and ventilation shafts were fitted on the outside, hence its rather cluttered appearance.

LE VENTRE DE PARIS

The 'belly of Paris' was the evocative name given to the area in the 19th century by the novelist Émile Zola. At that time it had been the main food supply centre of the city for centuries, growing until it reached bursting point. The Pavillons Baltard, built between 1854 and 1866, gave the market a new lease of life. However, 100 years later the market area became congested again, and the 'belly' of Paris moved out of town to Rungis, just south of the city.

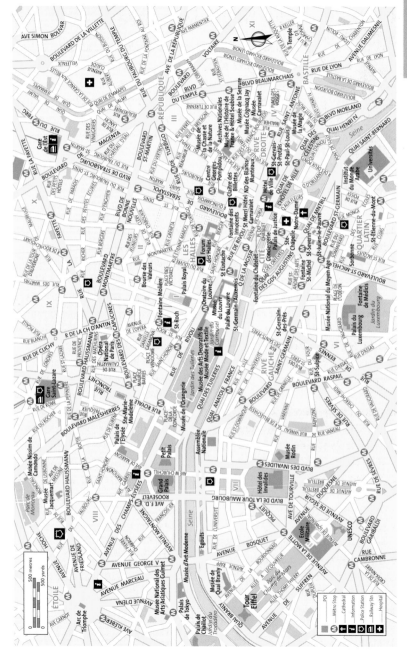

There is a public information library with French and foreign books, slides and films; an industrial design centre featuring architecture, town planning and industrial design; an acoustics and music research centre for the purpose of sound experimentation; a children's workshop; a cinema; an assortment of rooms for temporary exhibitions, concerts and lectures; and, of course, the Musée National d'Art Moderne.

A variety of tickets is available to the centre depending on what parts of the collection you want to see.

The museum

This is situated on the third and fourth floors; the entrance is on the fourth floor, which you can reach via the serpent-like escalator accessible from the main hall.

The collections of the former Musée d'Art Moderne, which retrace the

Pompidou Centre: something for everyone

evolution of art through the 20th century, were transferred from the Palais de Tokyo and have since been extended considerably to include contemporary art.

The third floor houses frequently renewed exhibits of abstract and figurative contemporary art from 1965 onwards, while the fourth floor displays all the major currents of modern art from 1905 to 1965. On this floor there are two main sections: on the south (St-Merri) side as you enter you can see the early 20th-century trends – Fauvism and Cubism – while on the north side the main post-World War I trends are represented.

On the south side the striking colours characteristic of Fauvism are illustrated in works by Derain, Vlaminck and, above all, Matisse, while Bonnard, whose work does not fit into the main trends, is also well represented.

There is a large selection of works by the main exponents of Cubism: Braque, Picasso, Gris and also Léger.

On the north side abstract art is represented by Mondrian, Kupka, Klee and Delaunay. The sombre, mystic style of Rouault and Chagall's world of fantasy dominate the 1920s and 1930s, alongside the Dada movement, which deliberately derided society.

Surrealism is well represented by Dalí, Magritte, Ernst, Miró and Masson; so is the CoBrA Group headed by Asger Jorn after World War II. The American school of Abstract Expressionism is strikingly represented by Pollock's

One of the four sphinxes that sit at the foot of the Fontaine du Châtelet

'drip-and-splash' style. The 1960s saw the advent of New Realism, and Pop Art flourished with Andy Warhol.

The fifth floor offers you a chance to relax in the pleasant cafeteria and enjoy beautiful views over the capital.
Place Georges Pompidou, 75004.
Tel: 01 44 78 12 33.
www.centrepompidou.fr.
Open: Wed–Mon 11am–9pm. Closed: Tue. Métro: Rambuteau, Châtelet & Hôtel de Ville.

Fontaine du Châtelet

This is one of the 15 fountains that Napoleon had built in the city. Dating from 1808, it is sometimes referred to as the Fontaine de la Victoire because it commemorates the emperor's victories in Italy and Egypt. Most often, though, it is called the Fontaine du Palmier because its column suggests a palm tree.
Place du Châtelet, 75001, near the Hôtel de Ville. Métro: Châtelet.

Fontaine des Innocents

This Renaissance fountain gets its name from the 12th-century Église Sts-Innocents demolished at the end of the 18th century. Built in 1550 at the corner of rue St-Denis by the architect Pierre Lescot and the sculptor Jean Goujon, it was later moved to the centre of the square and restored in 1865, when the original reliefs round the base were removed to the Louvre.
Rue Saint-Denis, 75001, near Les Halles. Métro: Les Halles or Châtelet.

Forum des Halles

There was a great deal of controversy in Paris about the destruction in 1972 of the 19th-century Pavillons Baltard, which housed the old market, for which Parisians suddenly discovered a deep attachment. Firmly rooted traditions were being threatened, they felt, and would be lost forever in the pursuit of improbable benefits. However, the planners won and work went ahead.

The originality of the resulting complex lies in the fact that there is little to be seen from the street: galleries on four levels run round a huge crater, which provides ample daylight in the central square. From there, a maze of underground 'streets', lined with shops, snack bars, cinemas and restaurants, and with direct access to the métro, covers an area of 7ha (17¼ acres); large maps are available on each level to direct you to the shops of your choice. On level one is a museum: the **Nouveau Musée Grévin**, an annexe of the waxworks in boulevard Montmartre (*see p80*), depicting Paris at the turn of the 20th century.

In the newest part of the complex, beyond place Carrée on level three, a cultural and commercial area includes an auditorium and a video library, as well as sports facilities and a glass swimming pool.

At ground level, round the gardens, which offer a pleasant contrast to the feverish underground activity, the old streets have preserved the character of the former market district, and many of the food shops, cafés and restaurants are still there.

Nearby Montorgueil is a lively street with vegetable stalls, cheese shops, bakeries and restaurants. While few tourists make it to this area, it is a haunt of Parisians shopping for good food.
Forum des Halles, 75001. Métro: Les Halles. RER: Châtelet.

Place du Châtelet

This was extensively remodelled by Haussmann, who commissioned two theatres from the architect Davioud: the Théâtre du Châtelet, where musicals, operas and concerts are still regularly staged; and the Théâtre de la Ville, once the Théâtre Sarah Bernhardt, where the famous actress delighted Parisians with her inspired performances.
Métro: Châtelet.

Rue Quincampoix

Situated near the Centre Pompidou, this old street was the scene, in 1720, of a famous scandal involving the Scottish financier John Law. He founded a bank, encouraged wild speculation, and the inevitable crash ruined thousands. There are some interesting old houses near the junction with rue des Lombards.
Métro: Châtelet or Rambuteau.

St-Eustache

This was the parish church of the Halles and, now that the old food market has gone, it can be seen from afar. In 1532 work started on an imposing Gothic building modelled on Notre-Dame and dedicated to St Eustace. Although it took over 100 years to build, the original plans were followed to the letter and it was a truly Gothic church that was consecrated in 1637. Unfortunately, the 18th-century neoclassical façade that replaced the original one has rather spoilt the overall effect. Many famous people are connected with St-Eustache: Richelieu and Molière were baptised within its walls, where the latter was also marrioed; buried there are the author La Fontaine, Colbert (Louis XIV's finance minister), and the composer Rameau. The dimensions of the building are even more impressive from the inside than the outside. Notice the unusual height of the double aisles, the fine vault and the stained-glass windows in the chancel, dating from 1631 and featuring St Eustace among the Apostles. The church is decorated with exceptional monuments and fine works of art, including *Les Pélerins d'Emmaüs*, an early Rubens; it also has a strong musical tradition.

St-Eustache: imposing inside and out

Place du Jour, 75001, next to the Forum des Halles. Open: daily 9am–7.30pm. Métro: Les Halles.

St-Merri

This is another late Gothic church, completed in 1612. The interior was considerably remodelled under Louis XV, and the only original features are the stained-glass windows in the chancel.

The composer Camille Saint-Saëns used to play on the 17th-century organ, and there are regular concerts in the summer.

Rue de la Verrerie, 75004. Open: daily 3–5pm. Métro: Hôtel de Ville or Châtelet.

MARAIS

This is one of the most authentic districts of Paris, with a wealth of 17th-century domestic architecture. It is also a lively area, where variety and contrasts make strolling along its picturesque streets a real pleasure.

Only 30 years ago the Marais seemed irretrievably to have sunk back into its murky beginnings. The name means marshy land and this is exactly what it was until, in the 13th century, various religious communities, including the Knights Templars, turned it into arable land. In the late 15th century the Hôtel de Sens was built in rue du Figuier. Today it is one of the area's few remaining medieval residences. Notice the turrets and the beautiful courtyards. At the beginning of the 17th century

Henri IV had place Royale (now place des Vosges) built right at the heart of the district, and the aristocracy promptly commissioned the most renowned architects to design the splendid mansions (*hôtels*) seen there today. This was the Marais's golden age. But then fashion changed and the district, deserted by the wealthy in favour of Faubourg St-Germain, was taken over by shopkeepers and craftsmen, while the beautiful mansions gradually became dilapidated.

In the early 1960s the Culture Minister, André Malraux, made the district a protected area and restoration work began immediately. The Marais assumed its cultural heritage while offering its inhabitants a new quality of life. Some *hôtels* were cleverly converted into flats or turned into museums, and new shopkeepers moved in and set up smart boutiques. An artistic revival followed, which is still very apparent.

It is certainly worth taking your time, and even losing your way, in the side streets north of rue des Francs Bourgeois. There are also lively streets, which you don't want to miss. Stretching from one end of the Marais to the other, rue des Francs Bourgeois is a commercial street lined with many fine houses, boutiques, cafés and restaurants. Rue des Archives is well known for its leather goods and jewellery. Rue Vieille-du-Temple has an assortment of restaurants, cafés and quaint shops, and rue des Rosiers is the picturesque main street of the Jewish Quarter. South of the wide rue St-Antoine, the area of rue St-Paul and Village St-Paul is a must for antiques lovers.

Rue des Francs Bourgeois

Its medieval name, referring to the almshouses built in the 14th century for the non tax-paying citizens or *francs bourgeois*, and the house of Jean Hérouët (No 54) both recall the days when this street was the centre of the weaving trade. Today it is lined with 17th- and 18th-century mansions, boutiques and restaurants, such as L'Orée du Marais at No 29.

Hôtel de Soubise

Nestled at the corner of rue des Archives and rue des Francs Bourgeois this early 18th-century former residence

A new lease of life is being enjoyed by the mansions in the Marais

Façade of an old café, Musée Carnavalet

still displays corbelled turrets that are a reminder of the original 14th-century manor house beneath. Since 1808 it has been the home of the National Archives. Included among several beautiful old residences in the surrounding area is the **Hôtel de Lamoignon,** one of the oldest mansions in the district, built in 1584.

Musée de L'Histoire de France This museum, housed in the beautiful Hôtel de Soubise, depicts French history through documents from the National Archives. Of particular interest are: the Edit de Nantes of 1598 recognising religious freedom, and its Révocation in 1685, which led to the exile of the Huguenots; the 1789 Déclaration des Droits de l'Homme (Declaration of Human Rights); Louis XVI's diary; and Napoleon's will. Princesse de Soubise's apartments have the most exquisite

rococo decorations, with paintings by Natoire, Boucher and Van Loo.
60 rue des Francs Bourgeois, 75003.
Tel: 01 40 27 60 96.
www.museehistoiredefrance.fr.
Open: Mon & Wed–Fri 10am–12.30pm & 2–5.30pm, Sat–Sun 2–5.30pm.
Closed: Tue. Admission charge.
Métro: Rambuteau.

Musée Carnavalet et de l'Histoire de Paris (Museum of the History of Paris)

Located in rue de Sévigné, the **Hôtel Carnavalet** is a Renaissance mansion, which was remodelled by Mansart in the 17th century. Madame de Sévigné lived in it for 20 years and wrote many of her famous letters there. Today it houses the **Musée Carnavalet – Histoire de Paris,** which was recently extended to the Hôtel Le-Peletier-de-St-Fargeau, and covers the history of Paris from its origins to the present day. The Hôtel Carnavalet section of the museum is reached through the monumental doorway and across the courtyard with its equestrian statue of Louis XIV by Coysevox. There are some interesting scenes from 16th-century Paris life, supported by a host of details such as shop and inn signs. Upstairs are reconstructed rooms from the reigns of Louis XIV, XV and XVI, and Madame de Sévigné's apartments.

The Hôtel Le-Peletier-de-St-Fargeau is linked to the Hôtel Carnavalet, and covers the period from the French Revolution; start on the second floor.

There are models of the Bastille and the guillotine, and everyday objects, as well as a reconstruction of the Temple prison where Louis XVI was held. The ground floor deals with the first half of the 19th century through portraits of people in the limelight. The first floor follows on with the Second Empire and the great architectural schemes that were carried out during that period. The lifestyle of the early 20th century is presented through reconstructions of rooms such as Marcel Proust's bedroom.
23 rue de Sévigné, 75003. Tel: 01 44 59 58 58. www.carnavalet.paris.fr. Open: Tue–Sun 10am–5.30pm. Closed: Mon. Admission charge. Métro: St-Paul.

Cloître des Billettes

Built in the 15th century as part of a monastery, this is the only medieval cloister left in Paris. The church next door dates from the 18th century.
24 rue des Archives. Tel: 01 42 72 38 79.

Musée de la Chasse et de la Nature (Museum of Hunting and Nature)

In rue des Archives the **Hôtel Guénégaud**, built in 1650, houses the Musée de la Chasse et de la Nature, which has a collection of arms as well as pictures by Vernet, Oudry and Chardin, and tapestries based on the theme of hunting.
60 rue des Archives. Tel: 01 53 01 92 40. www.chassenature.org. Open: daily

11am–5.15pm (later in summer). Admission charge. Métro: Hôtel de Ville.

Musée Cognacq-Jay

This collection of 18th-century art has found a proper setting in the recently renovated Hôtel Donon in the Marais. Paintings and pastels by Boucher, Fragonard, La Tour, Greuze, Tiepolo and Reynolds, and drawings by Watteau, are enhanced by fine pieces of furniture and other objects of the same period.
8 rue Elzévir, 75003. Tel: 01 40 27 07 21. Open: Tue–Sun 10am–5.30pm. Closed: Mon. Admission charge. Métro: St-Paul.

Musée de la Magie

This museum of magic and curiosities spreads through several cellar-like rooms and is great fun for children and adults alike. There are live magic shows as well as a wonderful shop.
11 rue St Paul, 75004. Tel: 01 42 72 13 26. www.museedelamagie.com. Open: Wed & Sat–Sun 2–7pm. Closed: Mon–Tue & Thur–Fri. Admission charge. Métro: St-Paul.

Musée de la Serrure (Lock Museum)

Housed in the home of the architect who built the Invalides, the museum's collection traces the history of locks since Roman times.
1 rue de la Perle. Tel: 01 42 77 79 62. Open: Mon–Fri 10am–noon & 2–5pm. Closed: Sat–Sun. Admission charge. Métro: St-Paul.

Notre-Dame-des-Blancs-Manteaux

This church is famous for its woodwork, in particular its rococo pulpit and organ loft. Concerts are given here during the Marais festival. *12 rue des Blancs-Manteaux. Métro: St-Paul.*

Place des Vosges

This beautiful square is sober, yet its extremely refined architecture gives it a kind of exquisite charm.

Commissioned by Henri IV at the beginning of the 17th century, the square was inaugurated after his death by his son Louis XIII and named place Royale. The two higher buildings, in the centre of the south and north sides, are called Pavillon du Roi (King's Pavilion) and Pavillon de la Reine (Queen's Pavilion) respectively, though they were never inhabited by the royal family. In the central garden stands a statue of Louis XIII. The square was renamed place des Vosges in 1800.

Some of the other residences have been lived in by famous people: Madame de Sévigné was born at No 1 bis in 1626, Cardinal Richelieu occupied No 21 before he moved to the Palais Royal and Victor Hugo lived in No 6 from 1832 to 1848, before his exile to Jersey and Guernsey. **Maison de Victor Hugo** is now a museum with various mementoes of his life: furniture, objects he collected, portraits and photographs, and also drawings by Hugo himself.

Maison de Victor Hugo, 6 place des Vosges, 75004. Tel: 01 42 72 10 16. Open: Tue–Sun 10am–6pm. Closed: Mon. Permanent collection: free admission. Admission charge for temporary exhibitions. Métro: St-Paul.

St-Gervais-St-Protais

Dedicated to two Roman officers martyred under Nero, this church offers an interesting contrast of styles: the main part is late Gothic with a three-tiered classical façade. Inside there are beautifully carved stalls, 16th- and 17th-century stained glass and a fine 17th-century organ.

Place St-Gervais, 75004. Open: Mon–Fri 6am–9pm & Sat–Sun 7am–9pm. Métro: Hôtel de Ville.

Maison de Victor Hugo, place des Vosges

The historic centre

Walk: Beaubourg and Forum des Halles

Major redevelopment gave this district a new lease of life in the 1970s and today the area attracts a crowd of young trendsetters, while the gastronomic tradition has been maintained by the score of small restaurants that once surrounded the old food market.

Allow 2 hours (excluding a visit to the Georges Pompidou Centre).

Coming out of the Hôtel de Ville métro station, follow avenue Victoria and turn right into rue St-Martin.

1 Tour St-Jacques

The Tour St-Jacques on the left is all that remains of the 16th-century church of St-Jacques-de-la-Boucherie, a starting point for pilgrims bound for Santiago de Compostela. Nearby there is a statue of Pascal, who conducted barometric experiments in the tower.
Continue along rue St-Martin.

2 Around St-Merri

The names of the streets surrounding the late-Gothic church of St-Merri recall their association with medieval trades. There is rue de la Verrerie (glassmakers) alongside the church and, opposite, rue des Lombards, named after the family who set themselves up as moneylenders. The rue St-Martin is lined with shops and bistros. On the north side of the church, the intrusion of the 20th century is emphasised by the colourful fountain in the middle of place Igor Stravinsky.
Just north of the place is the Centre Georges Pompidou (see pp22–5).

3 Centre Georges Pompidou

Although used to designate the Centre Pompidou, Beaubourg is the name of the old district that has come into the limelight following the success of the cultural centre. North of the centre lies the Quartier de l'Horloge: a lively pedestrianised area of narrow streets and arcades, with numerous shops and a curious modern clock called Le Défenseur du Temps (the Defender of Time), in rue Bernard de Clairvaux.
Return to the place Igor Stravinsky and turn right into the rue Aubry le Boucher.

4 Forum des Halles

Rest awhile in place J du Bellay: it has the most beautiful Renaissance fountain. The neat gardens have replaced the old food market – gone underground. Escalators lead down into the Forum, a multi-level entertainment and shopping centre (*see pp25–6*).

Come up on the rue Rambuteau side and walk to the church of St-Eustache (see pp26–7), then round the north side of it for the best views.

5 Bourse du Commerce

As you leave rue du Jour you can see the Bourse du Commerce in front of you; it replaced the city's corn exchange in 1889. To the right is rue Coquillière,

lined with restaurants including the famous Au Pied de Cochon.

At the end of rue J J Rousseau, turn left into rue St-Honoré.

6 Oratoire du Louvre

See p40.

Turn right into rue de l'Amiral de Coligny to reach the embankment; the church of St-Germain-l'Auxerrois (see pp43–4) offers an interesting mixture of styles. Return to place du Châtelet and its impressive fountain along quai de la Mégisserie.

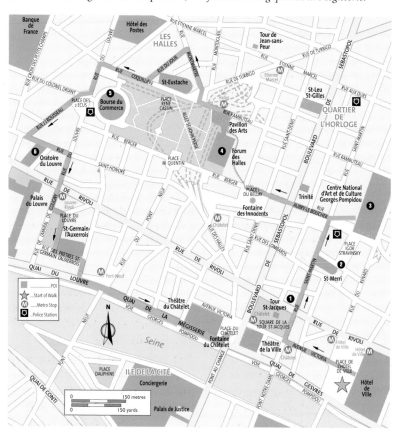

St-Gervais-St-Protais

St-Paul-St-Louis

This Baroque church, which was completed in 1641, was modelled on the Gesù church in Rome. The interior is well lit and richly decorated; in the transept there is a *Christ au Jardin des Oliviers* by Delacroix.
7 Passage St-Paul, 75004. Tel: 01 42 72 30 32. Métro: St-Paul.

Rue François Miron

One of the first roads to cross the marshy area or *marais*, the street is lined with old houses of interest: Nos 11 and 13 are half-timbered, 15th-century houses; Nos 44 to 46 have splendid Gothic cellars; and, further up, the 17th-century Hôtel de Beauvais (No 68) rang with Mozart's music

when the young prodigy stayed there in 1763. The Baroque church of St-Paul-St-Louis stands at the beginning of rue St-Antoine.

Rue St-Antoine

This has been the main street of the Marais since the 14th century, when it was a favourite venue for jousting contests. Henri II was fatally wounded here in 1559 in a tournament to celebrate his daughter's wedding. The courtyard of the 1625 Hôtel de Sully (No 62) has impressive sculptures featuring the seasons and the elements.

LOUVRE AND RIVOLI
Concorde

Place de la Concorde, or la Concorde as it is simply called, is undoubtedly the most splendid square in Paris. Its impressive size, harmonious proportions and superbly elegant setting are the striking features of this true masterpiece of town planning. Because of its strategic position at the crossroads of the main east–west and north–south flows of traffic, it gets very congested at times.

The square was commissioned by the aldermen of Paris as a token of their admiration for Louis XV. Ambitious plans submitted by the architect Jacques-Ange Gabriel were approved and a vast area of more than 8ha (20 acres) of drained marshland was chosen on the edge of town.

Built over a period of 20 years from 1755 to 1775, Place Louis XV was originally surrounded by a moat and balustrade, and an equestrian statue of the King by Bouchardon was placed in its centre.

Before work was completed tragedy struck: in 1770 a huge crowd had gathered on the square to celebrate the wedding of Marie-Antoinette and the future Louis XVI, when panic caused more than 100 people to be crushed to death in the moat.

Twenty-two years later the guillotine was set up on the square, which had been renamed place de la Révolution. In 1795 the dreaded instrument was dismantled and the square renamed place de la Concorde as a symbol of hope and peace!

It was not until 1836 that the name was adopted for good. The square was partly redesigned by the architect Hittorff and the decoration completed. King Louis-Philippe decided against another statue in the centre and chose instead a neutral monument – a 3,000-year-old Egyptian obelisk.

The obelisk

The obelisk, which comes from the temple of Luxor, was a gift from the viceroy of Egypt, Muhammad Ali. This imposing pink granite monolith, 23m (75ft) high and weighing 220 tonnes, is 3,300 years old. It is covered with hieroglyphs that detail the life of Rameses II, and the drawings on the base depict the process of dismantling and transporting it, and erecting it on its present site. The two large fountains are modelled on those in St Peter's Square in Rome.

One of the enormous fountains in la Concorde

The views from the centre of the square are magnificent. To the west are the Champs-Élysées and the Arc de Triomphe, to the east the Jardin des Tuileries, the Arc de Triomphe du Carrousel and the Louvre beyond, to the north rue Royale, closed off by the Madeleine, and to the south Pont de la Concorde and the Assemblée Nationale across the river.

The twin mansions

The colonnades of the two identical buildings marking the entrance to rue Royale were modelled on that of the Louvre. Hôtel de la Marine is on the right as you face the Madeleine, and Hôtel Crillon is on the left. This is now a world-famous luxury hotel, but in 1778, soon after it was built, it was the venue for the signing of an important treaty between France and the newly founded United States of America.

Statues round the square

To complete the decoration, eight statues representing various French towns stand in the corners of the square. Outside the Tuileries' gates are two figures on winged horses by Coysevox, representing Fame and Mercury. To complement them the famous *Chevaux de Marly* by Coustou were brought from Louis XIV's castle to mark the entrance to the Champs-Élysées. Both the sets now displayed are replicas, as the marble originals have been taken to the Louvre.

Fontaine Molière

Situated at the intersection of rues de Richelieu and Molière, this fountain is dedicated to the famous 17th-century playwright who died at No 40 rue de Richelieu. Built by Visconti in 1844, it shows the writer deeply absorbed in his thoughts.
Rue de Richelieu, 75001, near the Palais Royal.
Métro: Palais-Royal or Pyramides.

Hôtel de Ville (City Hall)

Although the present building is fairly recent, the site has always played an essential role in the history of the capital. In the Middle Ages the square in front of the town hall was called the place de Grève because it sloped down to the river (*grève* means shore as well as strike). Throughout the Ancien Régime the site was used for public executions. In 1871, during the Commune uprising, the original town hall was destroyed by fire at the same time as the Tuileries Palace.

The present building, which is in neo-Renaissance style, dates from 1882. Its decoration is very elaborate, as was the fashion at the turn of the 20th century: numerous statues adorn the façade, and inside, at the top of a splendid staircase, there are reception rooms with beautiful crystal chandeliers and paintings.
4 place de l'Hôtel de Ville, 75004.
Tel: 01 42 76 40 40. www.paris.fr.
Free guided tours by appointment only (Mon–Fri). Entrance by the north door.
Métro: Hôtel de Ville.

Musée des Arts Décoratifs (Museum of Decorative Arts) and Musée de la Mode et du Textile (Fashion and Textile Museum)

The collections of the Arts Décoratifs are presented chronologically in the north wing of the Louvre. The 20th-century section includes a splendid reconstruction of Jeanne Lanvin's flat, some Dubuffet paintings and sculptures, and glass objects by Gallé and Lalique. There is also a large toy collection.

The Fashion and Textile Museum charts the history of fashion from the Middle Ages to the present day.
107 rue de Rivoli, 75001. Tel: 01 44 55 59 26. www.lesartsdecoratifs.fr.

Open: Tue–Sun 11am–6pm (until 9pm Thur). Closed: Mon. Admission charge. Métro: Palais-Royal or Tuileries.

Musée du Louvre

François I started the royal collection in the 16th century by acquiring 12 paintings by Italian masters, which included Leonardo da Vinci's *Mona Lisa* – housed in the Denon wing and still the most famous of the museum's art treasures. During the reign of Louis XIV, the king's minister, Colbert, practised a policy of systematic buying, and the collection swelled to more than 2,000 paintings.

The historic centre

Hôtel de Ville

The pyramid is illuminated at night

Meanwhile the Académie Royale de Peinture et de Sculpture, founded in 1648, was already holding its annual exhibition in the Louvre and artists were granted lodgings in the palace. Shortly after the creation of the museum in 1793 works of art were brought back from Versailles, and later Napoleon and his successors continued to enrich the collections with Greek, Assyrian and Egyptian antiquities.

The Louvre consists of three wings, Sully, Denon and Richelieu, which house the museum's seven departments, identifiable by a colour code. The collections are displayed on four levels, each divided into ten *arrondissements* accessible by means of escalators from the underground reception area, where leaflets in English (including ground plans) are available to help you decide what you want to see. There are also maps and signposts throughout the museum. If you are looking for a particular work then ask a member of staff to direct you, in case there has been a rearrangement of exhibits.

Sully

The medieval moat The Sully escalator leads directly to rooms depicting the history of the palace and surrounding area; from there you can go to the Sully region, or walk round the moat of the medieval fortress buried under the Cour Carrée. Objects found during the excavations include Charles VI's gilt helmet (14th century).

Oriental antiquities This department houses archaeological finds from the valleys of the Euphrates and the Tigris, concerning mainly the Sumerian and Babylonian civilisations, the Elamite and Persian civilisations, the Phoenicians and the Assyrians.

Egyptian antiquities The great Sphinx in pink granite makes a most impressive introduction to Egyptian art, while the Seated Scribe, dating from around 2500 BC, and the bust of Amenophis IV from Karnak are strikingly realistic masterpieces.

Paintings The second floor of the Sully wing hosts the French school

The historic centre

of painters, strongly represented by de la Tour, Poussin, Watteau, Delacroix and Géricault.

Denon
Greek, Etruscan and Roman antiquities You cannot visit the Louvre without seeing the 2nd-century BC sculpture of Venus de Milo, generally acknowledged as a perfect example of feminine beauty.

Paintings This wing also hosts the Italian and Spanish collections of paintings. Among the most outstanding works of the Italian school are pieces by Leonardo da Vinci, Titian and Raphael.

One of the many treasures from the Louvre's sculpture collections

Sculpture The lower ground and ground floors of the Denon wing play host to Italian, Spanish and Northern European sculpture.

Richelieu
Paintings Several paintings by Flemish and Dutch painters, including Rembrandt and Van Dyck, are to be found on the second floor of this wing.

Sculpture French sculpture is displayed on the lower ground floor of the Richelieu wing, in the Marly and Puget sculpture courts. Of special interest are *Les Nymphes* by Jean Goujon and *Les Chevaux de Marly* by Guillaume Coustou, a copy of which guards the entrance to the Champs-Élysées.

Musée du Louvre, Palais du Louvre, 75001, Paris. Tel: 01 40 20 51 77. www.louvre.fr. Open: Thur & Sat–Mon 9am–6pm; Wed & Fri 9am–10pm. Closed: Tue. Admission charge. Facilities: bookshop, audio guides, auditorium, and restaurant and cafeteria that stay open after closing time. Main entrance under the glass pyramid in the Cour Napoléon. Métro: Palais-Royal.

In order to avoid unnecessary delays, use the direct access from the Palais-Royal métro station to the museum through the Carrousel du Louvre, a vast underground architectural complex that forms part of the Grand Louvre Project and links the Jardin des Tuileries to the Louvre. It includes the

Galerie du Carrousel, a wide alleyway lit at one end by an inverted glass pyramid and leading to the museum's entrance hall.

Musée National de l'Orangerie (Orangerie Museum)

A substantial collection of paintings from the Impressionist period to the early 20th century is housed here, but it is mostly renowned for Monet's *Nymphéas* (Water Lilies).

There are also some remarkable still lifes by Cézanne, some delightful portraits by Renoir and paintings by Picasso, Derain, Modigliani and Matisse, as well as a few of Henri Rousseau's best naive works, including *La Carriole du Père Junier*.

Monet's huge *Nymphéas*, painted at Giverny, are exhibited on the ground floor in two oval rooms, according to the instructions given by the artist himself.

Place de la Concorde, 75001. Tel: 01 44 77 80 07. www.musee-orangerie.fr. Open: Wed–Mon 9am–6pm. Closed: Tue. Admission charge. Métro: Concorde.

Oratoire du Louvre

This 17th-century church by Le Mercier was used as the royal chapel under Louis XIII, Louis XIV and Louis XV, who listened to the sermons of famous preachers such as Bossuet. After the revolution of 1789 it became a Protestant church.

1 rue de l'Oratoire, 75001. Tel: 01 42 60 21 64. Métro: Louvre-Rivoli.

THE COMÉDIE-FRANÇAISE

This famous theatre company was founded by Louis XIV in 1680, a few years after Molière's death, with the aim of combining two rival theatre companies. Frowned upon by the Sorbonne, it was forced to move several times until Napoleon made it an official institution with a director appointed by the State. Its repertoire is traditionally classical, but also includes works by modern authors, both French and foreign. In the foyer is the chair that Molière collapsed into during a performance of *Le Malade Imaginaire*.

Palais du Louvre

Situated on the right bank, within a stone's throw of the Île de la Cité, the Palais du Louvre expanded according to the whim of successive French monarchs, and today it is one of the world's largest royal palaces. It is better known, however, for the great museum within its walls. The 'Grand Louvre' project was designed to modernise and smarten it up, and the eye-catching glass pyramid erected in the open courtyard renewed interest in the building's 'threatened' architectural beauty.

The original castle was consistently extended westwards, away from the congested part of the city. Built by King Philippe-Auguste at the end of the 12th century, the Louvre castle was just a massive keep surrounded by a wall and towers, designed as part of the city's fortifications. It became a royal residence when Charles V extended the city and protected it with new fortifications. Remains of this fortress were discovered under the Cour Carrée, and have been excavated recently as part of the Grand Louvre scheme (access through the museum).

Until the 16th century the Louvre was neglected in favour of less austere residences in the Marais or on the Loire; then François I had part of the obsolete fortress razed, and in 1546 he commissioned Pierre Lescot to build a new palace. Lescot worked on it until his death in 1571, entrusting the decoration to the sculptor Jean Goujon.

Catherine de' Medici, Henri II's widow, initiated the extension of the Louvre westwards. She commissioned Philibert Delorme to build a new palace close to the Louvre, known as the **Tuileries**. However, superstition prevented her from settling in it – an astrologer told her she would die there. In 1871 it was burned down and had to be demolished.

Catherine de' Medici also originally had intended to link the two palaces by way of a long wing, but these plans were abandoned until Henri IV's accession to the throne. He completed the link in 1608 by having the **Galerie du Bord de l'Eau (Waterside Gallery)** and the Pavillon de Flore built.

Louis XIII and Louis XIV concentrated their efforts on the **Cour Carrée**. In 1624 the architect Lemercier built the **Pavillon de l'Horloge (Clock Pavillion)** in the centre of the west wing, which he extended by another building faithfully matching that of Pierre Lescot. The other three sides

The magnificent Palais du Louvre, home to the famous museum

were completed by Louis XIV's architects: Le Vau, Le Brun and Perrault, who also rebuilt the Apollo wing linking the Cour Carrée to the Galerie du Bord de l'Eau. The impressive Colonnade marks the formal entrance to the palace.

Abandoned in favour of Versailles at the end of the 17th century, the palace was neglected and taken over by artists and their families; eventually an assortment of buildings concealed the beautiful façades, which were threatened with dilapidation. However, in 1793 the Galerie du Bord de l'Eau was turned into a museum.

Napoleon settled in the Tuileries and restored order to the architectural jumble; he also commissioned Percier and Fontaine to build the **Arc de Triomphe du Carrousel** and a north wing along rue de Rivoli, which Napoleon III completed.

The 'Grand Louvre' project was begun in 1981. Its purpose was to create more room for the museum by refurbishing the north wing (the Richelieu wing) formerly occupied by the French Exchequer, and to provide badly needed public facilities. The well-known American architect I M Pei consequently designed a vast new underground entrance hall over which stands a glass pyramid. The project was completed in 1999.

Palais Royal

The palace was commissioned in 1624 by Richelieu, who was then Louis XIII's minister. It became a *palais royal* (royal palace) when he left it to the king in his will. Louis XIV then gave it to his brother, Philippe d'Orléans, whose descendants surrounded the garden with elegant shopping arcades and apartments and built the Comédie-Française. Cafés, restaurants, gambling houses and dance halls thrived within its precinct until, in the mid-19th century, Louis-Philippe took the fun out of the area by closing the gambling houses.

The palace is not open to the public but you can go through the main courtyard, invaded by the black and white Colonnes de Buren (pillars), into the peaceful garden surrounded by dainty boutiques.
Place du Palais Royal.
Métro: Palais-Royal.

Place Vendôme

Built at the end of the 17th century by Jules Hardouin-Mansart, this imposing square is a magnificent example of the Louis XIV style.

Here, again, symmetry is the overriding principle: a terrace of mansions over a row of arcades, with an original feature designed to break the monotony. The central buildings and those cutting the four corners are surmounted by pediments. Chopin died at No 12, and No 15 is now the prestigious Ritz Hotel; famous jewellers are established all round the square.

The central column that replaced the equestrian statue of Louis XIV was erected by Napoleon to celebrate his victory at Austerlitz.

The statue at the top was changed many times until the Third Republic finally settled on a copy of the original, representing Napoleon dressed as a Roman.

Métro: Tuileries or Opéra.

Place des Victoires

The original statue of Louis XIV was installed by a rich admirer of the king, who subsequently had the square designed by Mansart to match the statue. Recently renovated, the square has attracted several well-known fashion boutiques.

Métro: Bourse or Palais-Royal.

St-Germain-l'Auxerrois

The church was built in the 12th century, but has been continually remodelled for 400 years. As a result it has a Romanesque belfry, a Gothic chancel and a late Gothic porch, while the aisle round the chancel is Renaissance. It is unfortunately associated with one of the darkest episodes of French history. In 1572 its bells gave the signal for the Massacre of St Bartholomew, when thousands of Protestants were murdered as a result of a plot between the Cardinal of Lorraine, the Duke of Guise, Catherine de' Medici, Charles IX and the future Henri III. Inside there are some interesting works of art, including a

Stunning window, St-Germain-l'Auxerrois

16th-century Flemish reredos in the fourth chapel on the left of the nave, 15th-century stained glass in the transept and the rose windows, and a polychrome statue of St Germain in front of the chancel.

Place du Louvre, 75001. Open: daily 8am–7pm. Métro: Louvre.

St-Roch

St-Roch is a fine example of classical architecture. Its foundation stone was laid by Louis XIV in 1653, but work was delayed through lack of funds and it was not completed until the 18th century. The façade, which is in the Jesuit style, dates from 1735. In 1795 Napoleon charged a group of royalist rebels here. The bullet holes can still be seen on the façade.

The classical façade of St-Roch

THE BUTTE ST-ROCH

The church of St-Roch was originally built on a hillock upon which stood several windmills. The butte was levelled off as part of Baron Haussmann's ambitious town-planning programme and the windmills all disappeared, except one – the Moulin Radet. This was removed to another high position, the Butte Montmartre, where you can still see it, in rue Lepic.

Rue St-Honoré, 75001. Open: Mon–Sat 8am–7pm. Closed: Sun except 5–6.30pm. Métro: Pyramides or Tuileries.

ÎLE DE LA CITÉ

It is no coincidence that the history of Paris began on this small, boat-shaped island in the middle of the Seine. Although the river has lost its once essential role, this tiny strip of land, known as the Île de la Cité, has remained the heart of the great metropolis that developed around it.

Lutetia was the name given to the city by the first known settlers, the Parisii: it was a Celtic word meaning 'a dwelling surrounded by water'.

The Romans brought organisation and prosperity, but after the fall of the Roman Empire the small island was in peril once again. Although it miraculously escaped the Huns, the Franks besieged it and eventually conquered it. When King Clovis made it his capital in 508 it became known as the 'Cité'. Its renewed prosperity attracted attention and it was soon threatened by Norman raids. The city was sacked several times until Eudes, Count of Paris, reinforced its fortifications and successfully defended it in 885. For more than 100 years afterwards, however, the town remained within the perimeter of the island.

As a centre of learning the cathedral played an essential role in maintaining the influence of the Cité after the town began to spread along the banks of the river. Schools flourished between the north side of Notre-Dame and the Seine, an area that belonged to the canons of the cathedral. Abélard was among the many students drawn to the Cité by the reputation of its teaching, and it was in the cloister school that he first met Héloïse (*see box, p52*). By the end of the 13th century there were a total of 22 chapels and churches near the cathedral.

Île de la Cité, ancient heart of Paris

From the 14th century onwards the kings of France ceased to live in the Cité, preferring the Louvre and other royal residences outside Paris. The royal palace became the seat of the Supreme Court of Justice. During the Terror, the dreaded *Tribunal révolutionnaire* held its sessions there, next door to the notorious Conciergerie.

The island has changed considerably since the Middle Ages, but its most spectacular remodelling took place during the second half of the 19th century. It was during that time that the area round the cathedral was cleared and began to look as it does today.

Conciergerie

This is the oldest part of the former royal palace, bordering the Seine along the quai de l'Horloge. It gets its name from the *concierge* (caretaker) who looked after the royal residence and was allowed to levy taxes. The building already served as a prison before the Revolution, and during the Terror it held such famous prisoners as Marie-Antoinette and Danton. Guided tours take you through the Salle des Gardes and the impressive Salle des Gens d'Armes with superb Gothic vaulting to the vast kitchens, the Galerie des Prisonniers and Marie-Antoinette's cell.

Conciergerie, 2 blvd du Palais, 75001. Tel: 01 53 40 60 80. Open: daily 9.30am–6pm. Admission charge. Métro: Cité.

Walk: Île de la Cité and Île St-Louis

This is the heart of medieval Paris: the bustling Île de la Cité with Notre-Dame Cathedral solidly camped at its eastern end and, next to it, the smaller, quieter, Île Saint-Louis.

Allow 2–3 hours.

From St-Michel métro station cross the Pont St-Michel, then turn right along the quai du Marché Neuf.

1 Place du Parvis Notre-Dame

Across this vast square, created by Haussmann, stands the austere Gothic cathedral (*see pp48–9*). Gallo-Roman and medieval remains are displayed in the Crypte Archéologique, beneath the Parvis. On the south side of the square stands the statue of Charlemagne.
Coming out of the cathedral, turn right along the north side.

2 The old cloister quarter

The rue Chanoinesse gives a fair idea of what the area looked like in the 13th century. It was here that the canons lived and taught; original houses at Nos 22 and 24 bring to mind the moving story of Héloïse and Abélard (*see box, p52*).
Turn left along quai de la Corse, then left into rue de la Cité and right into rue de Lutèce.

3 Place Louis Lépine

During the week the square is the site of a colourful flower market, and on Sundays a no less picturesque but somewhat noisier bird market takes place.
Continue along rue de Lutèce.
Facing are the Palais de Justice, the law courts, and the Sainte-Chapelle. Turn right, then left along quai de l'Horloge, past the Conciergerie, to reach place Dauphine.

4 Place Dauphine

This is a haven of peace where you can admire two of the original 17th-century brick-and-stone houses at Nos 12 and 14. Beyond the statue of Henri IV is the square du Vert Galant, which affords beautiful views of the river.
Cross over to the left bank, turn left and follow the embankment, lined with bookstalls, past Notre-Dame, then cross the Pont de l'Archevêché and the Pont St-Louis and turn left into quai de Bourbon.

5 Quai de Bourbon

Île Saint-Louis offers a peaceful village atmosphere, nowhere more apparent than along the cobbled quai de Bourbon, lined with classical mansions.

Continue along quai d'Anjou to No 17.

6 Hôtel de Lauzun

Built by Le Vau in 1657, the Hôtel de Lauzun, with its gilded-dolphin waterspouts, has had many famous occupants, including the poet Charles Pierre Baudelaire, who wrote much of *Les Fleurs du Mal* here, and the composer Wagner. The building now belongs to the City of Paris.

Further on along quai d'Anjou, turn right into rue St-Louis-en-l'Île.

7 Rue St-Louis-en-l'Île

This is the main street of the island. The 17th-century church of St-Louis-en-l'Île has an unusual clock outside and a richly decorated interior. A few doors away, at No 31, is the ice cream specialist Berthillon.

Turn left into rue des Deux Ponts, then cross the bridge. Facing you is the famous but expensive restaurant, La Tour d'Argent, and on your left the modern Institut du Monde Arabe (see p52). Turn right and follow the embankment back to place St-Michel.

Walk: Île de la Cité and Île St-Louis

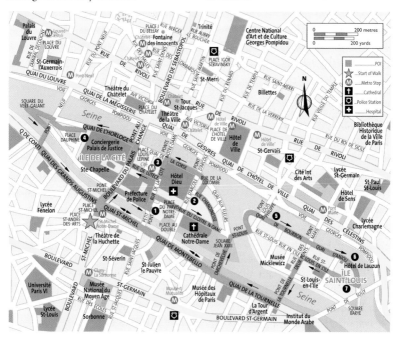

The historic centre

Notre-Dame

The harmonious strength of the cathedral's outline, the proportions of its façade and the subtle combination of simplicity and refinement in its design are undoubtedly the perfect expression of French Gothic architecture. Notre-Dame is the nucleus around which the capital developed, and major celebrations, often marking a turning point in French history, were staged in the cathedral.

In 1163 Bishop de Sully launched the building process that lasted nearly 200 years. The architects, Jean de Chelles and Pierre de Montreuil, worked on it during the 13th century, when the Sainte-Chapelle (Holy Chapel) was also built. The building was completed in 1345 with the addition of flying buttresses surrounding the chancel.

Although the cathedral never suffered spectacular damage, by the mid-19th century it had been deprived of some of its magnificent sculptures and the edifice was in serious need of repair. Restoration work was carried out under the care of Viollet-le-Duc, and the cathedral regained its past splendour. Haussmann later widened the Parvis (square) in front of it to increase the dramatic effect of its unique setting.

Today two other vantage points, the square Jean XXIII behind the chancel and the square Viviani on the left bank, reveal the perfect proportions of the edifice, which is 130m (427ft) long and 49m (161ft) wide. Its towers rise to a height of 68m (223ft).

The façade

The façade is the most striking part of the building. The heavily restored central portal depicts the Last Judgement, and the upper part shows Christ surrounded by the celestial court. The portal of the Virgin on the left has a

The cathedral as it appears from the River Seine

particularly beautiful tympanum illustrating the coronation of the Virgin Mary. The sculptures on the portal of St Anne on the right are the oldest in the cathedral; the remarkable tympanum also shows the Virgin Mary with Bishop Maurice de Sully, founder of the cathedral, at her side. The lintel depicts scenes from the life of St Anne.

The rose window is more than 700 years old. Birds and demons were placed at the base of the towers by Viollet-le-Duc in true Gothic spirit.

The great bell in the south tower, weighing 13 tonnes, is heard only on special occasions. The view from the top is rewarding if you have the courage to climb the 386 steps. The portal on the south side has a 13th-century tympanum, which depicts the martyr St Stephen. The slightly earlier north portal by Jean de Chelles was adorned with a statue of the Virgin and Child, but the child is now missing.

The interior

The vast interior can accommodate up to 9,000 people. The 35m (115ft)-high nave is separated from the chancel by a wide transept, which has two magnificent rose windows.

The chancel was redecorated in the 17th century as the result of a vow made by Louis XIII if he were granted an heir. A *pietà* by Coysevox stands in the centre, flanked by statues of Louis XIII and Louis XIV. On the right of the chancel, the treasury houses some old relics including a fragment of the True Cross.

Place du Parvis Notre-Dame, 75004. Tel: 01 42 34 56 10. www.notredamedeparis.fr. Open: daily 8am–6.45pm (7.15pm weekends). Admission charge. Treasury open: Mon–Fri 9.30am–6pm, Sat 9.30am–6.30pm, Sun 1.30–6.30pm. Admission charge. Towers open: winter 10am–5.15pm, spring & autumn 9.30am–6pm, 9am–7.30pm in summer (till 11pm weekends). Admission charge for both. Métro: St-Michel or Cité. RER: St-Michel-Notre-Dame.

Palais de Justice

This part of the old royal palace, many times destroyed by fire and considerably extended in the 19th century, has completely lost its medieval aspect, but it is still worth walking across the main courtyard to the bustling Galerie Marchande, before visiting the Sainte-Chapelle and the Conciergerie.

Sainte-Chapelle, 4 boulevard du Palais, 75001. Open: daily 10am–5pm.

Sainte-Chapelle

The distinctive, 75m (246ft)-high spire in the sky reveals from a distance the presence of this jewel of Gothic architecture, partly hidden by the Palais de Justice buildings. In 1239 Louis IX, better known as St Louis, acquired the Crown of Thorns from the emperor of Constantinople, together with other precious relics including a fragment of the True Cross, and immediately decided to build a special shrine to house them in the courtyard of the royal palace. Pierre de Montreuil was entrusted with this delicate task. The Sainte-Chapelle was built in less than three years and consecrated in 1248. After the Revolution it was no longer used as a church, and the relics were

Notre-Dame at night

4

transferred to Notre-Dame where they are now kept in the Treasury.

In order to let in as much light as possible the vaulted roof is supported by thin pillars, which are separated by long, narrow, stained-glass windows 15m (49ft) high. A few buttresses help reinforce the structure, which appears to have no walls. The narrow edifice consists of two chapels, one above the other. The *chapelle basse* (lower chapel) is richly decorated, and its floor paved with tombstones. A spiral staircase leads to the *chapelle haute* (upper chapel), which appears wrapped in a blaze of light and colour. The huge stained-glass windows are undoubtedly the most striking feature: still mainly 13th-century, they are the oldest in Paris, depicting over 1,000 scenes from the Old and New Testaments in great detail.

4 blvd du Palais, 75004. Tel: 01 53 40 60 96. Open: daily 9.30am–6pm (summer); 10am–5pm (winter). Admission charge. Access through the Cour de Mai of the Palais de Justice. Métro: St-Michel or Cité.

QUARTIER LATIN

The Latin Quarter is one of the oldest districts of Paris, rich in traditions going back to the Middle Ages yet teeming with new ideas launched by its lively young population. Situated opposite Île de la Cité, the district spreads from the place St-Michel uphill to the Montagne Ste-Geneviève dominated by the Panthéon and the Sorbonne. A free and easy atmosphere pervades the whole area.

Roman public buildings were concentrated on the left bank, just across the river from Île de la Cité occupied by the Celts. Ruins of public baths were discovered next to the Hôtel de Cluny, and those of an amphitheatre in the vicinity of the Jardin des Plantes. At the end of the 3rd century hordes of barbarians burned down the whole left bank, halting development there for a long time.

In the 12th century several teachers and students broke away from the cathedral schools of the Île de la Cité and established themselves on the left bank. Their action soon led to the foundation of the University of Paris in 1215. Before the end of the 13th century there were several colleges on the Montagne Ste-Geneviève, welcoming students from the French provinces and from many other parts of Europe as well. These early European students spoke Latin – a practice that lasted until 1789.

Fontaine Cuvier

This very ornate fountain, representing a young woman with animals lying at her feet, is dedicated to Baron Georges Cuvier – the 19th-century zoologist who founded the study of comparative anatomy and palaeontology. Notice the crocodile turning its head round, something crocodiles apparently cannot do!

Corner of rue Linné and rue Cuvier, 75005, near the Jardin des Plantes. Métro: Jussieu or Monge.

Fontaine de Médicis

This is the most romantic fountain in Paris and one of the main attractions of the Jardin du Luxembourg. Built in 1624 by Salomon de Brosse for Marie de' Medici, Henri IV's widow, it is in the Italian style that was fashionable at the time.
Jardin du Luxembourg, 75006. Métro: Odéon. RER: Luxembourg.

Fontaine St-Michel

This monumental fountain was built by Davioud during the Second Empire and is typical of the ornate style in fashion at the time. It is a favourite meeting place for young Parisians.
Place St-Michel, 75005, in the Latin Quarter. Métro: St-Michel.

Institut du Monde Arabe (Arab World Institute)

The building situated by the river, facing the Île St-Louis, is the result of close cooperation between France and 19 Arab countries with the aim of promoting cultural exchanges between Islam and the West. The institute houses a reference centre, a video centre, a comprehensive library, research facilities and a museum (on the 7th floor) that illustrates Arab civilisation from the 9th century onwards. The south façade consists of 1,600 identical metal light

HÉLOÏSE AND ABÉLARD

A tragic love story unites the names of Canon Fulbert's niece Héloïse and a young teacher from Brittany called Abélard. About 100 years before the foundation of the Sorbonne, Abélard became Héloïse's tutor at her uncle's request. They fell in love, eloped, got married and had a son. When they returned to Paris Canon Fulbert decided to punish Abélard by having him castrated. Abélard became a monk and a famous teacher while Héloïse took the veil, but their love survived and they went on writing passionate letters to each other.

They were buried in the same grave inside the monastery that Abélard had founded, and of which Héloïse had subsequently become the abbess. Their remains were later transferred to the Cimetière du Père Lachaise.

screens that electronically filter the sunlight as it enters the building. From the cafeteria on the 9th floor there are lovely views of the river.
1 Rue des Fossés St-Bernard, 75005. Tel: 01 40 51 38 38. www.imarabe.org. Open: Tue–Sun 10am–6pm. Closed: Mon. Admission charge. Métro: Jussieu or Cardinal-Lemoine.

Musée National du Moyen Âge (Museum of the Middle Ages)

The museum is housed in two buildings, the Gallo-Roman Thermes de Cluny and the Hôtel de Cluny. It was founded in 1843 when Alexandre du Sommerard, a passionate collector who lived in the Hôtel de Cluny, donated his collections to the French State. The museum offers a unique perspective on life and the arts

from Gallo-Roman times to the
16th century.

Hôtel de Cluny

This is one of the best examples of
domestic medieval architecture. It was
built in the 15th century for the abbots
of the famous Cluny Abbey on the site
of the ruined Roman baths. The style
of the house is inspired by the
Renaissance, best observed from the
main courtyard. The central building
has high windows and an elaborate
balustrade with impressive gargoyles,
while the main staircase winds up a
pentagonal tower.

Musée National du Moyen Âge – Thermes de Cluny

On the ground floor there are 15th- and
16th-century tapestries made in Holland
in the *mille fleurs* style. Particularly
worthy of note is a set called *La Vie
Seigneuriale*, depicting the life of the
aristocracy in the 16th century.

In room VIII there are some
fragments of sculpture, including 21
heads from the Galerie des Rois that
were originally on the west front of
Notre-Dame. Next door is the well-
preserved *frigidarium* (cold bath) with
a fine example of Roman vaulting.

On the first floor is the museum's
major exhibit: a set of six tapestries
from the late 15th century, called
La Dame à la Licorne (the Lady and the
Unicorn). The lovely Gothic chapel
contains another set of tapestries
illustrating the life of St Stephen.

6 place Paul-Painlevé, 75005.
Tel: 01 53 73 78 16.
www.musee-moyenage.fr.
Open: Wed–Mon 9.15am–5.45pm.
Closed: Tue. Admission charge. Métro:
Cluny-La Sorbonne, St-Michel or Odéon.

Panthéon

This vast monument towering over the
Quartier Latin tends to dwarf
everything around it, particularly the
beautiful church of St-Étienne-du-
Mont. Looked at from a distance,
however, the harmonious proportions
of its high dome, underlined by an
elegant ring of slender columns,
make it a splendid example of
neoclassical architecture.

When, in 1744, Louis XV suffered a
serious illness he vowed to build a
beautiful new church to replace the

The façade of Paris's Panthéon

ancient Abbey of St Geneviève. After his recovery he commissioned the architect, Jacques Soufflot, who designed a magnificent building in the shape of a Greek cross, with a huge dome 83m (272ft) high; the saint's shrine would be placed beneath it. Work began in 1758 but was only completed after Soufflot's death in 1789 on the eve of the French Revolution.

Forty-two of the original windows were blocked up in 1791 and the bare walls were later decorated with scenes depicting the life of St Geneviève by Pierre Puvis de Chavannes, as well as paintings by other late 19th-century artists.

The same year the Assemblée Constituante decided that all the nation's 'great men' should be buried inside the church, which was renamed Panthéon after the Greek and Roman temples dedicated to all the gods. However, with the return of the monarchy the building became a church once again until, in 1885, the decision was finally taken to restore it to its role of national mausoleum, in honour of the writer Victor Hugo who had just died.

In the vast crypt are the tombs of some of France's 'great men': Voltaire, Rousseau, Hugo, Zola, the Resistance leader Jean Moulin, Jean Monnet, usually referred to as the 'father of Europe', and many others.

Place du Panthéon, 75005. Tel: 01 44 32 18 00. Open: daily 10am–6.30pm. Admission charge. Métro: Cardinal-Lemoine. RER: Luxembourg.

The lively, open-air market charms visitors to rue Mouffetard

Place de l'Odéon

This square has hardly altered since the late 18th century. The sober architecture of its houses contrasts with the Greek-temple style of the Théâtre National de l'Odéon dating from 1782. The Café Voltaire at No 1 was the meeting place of 18th-century philosophers, including Voltaire, Diderot and d'Alembert. It sadly no longer exists.
Métro: Odéon.

Rue Mouffetard

Running downhill from the top of Montagne Ste-Geneviève, rue Mouffetard (the 'Mouff') is one of the most picturesque streets in Paris. The bottom section is the liveliest, with its open-air market and the colourful shop signs creating a village-like atmosphere. A little way up, on either side, are passage des Postes and passage des Patriarches, both worth exploring, while further up still, on the left, rue du Pot-de-Fer has some interesting restaurants. The Fontaine du Pot-de-Fer, on the corner, was built in the 17th century and supplied by an aqueduct that brought water to the Palais du Luxembourg. The street ends at the charming place de la Contrescarpe.
75005. Métro: Monge or Censier-Daubenton.

Rue St-André-des-Arts

Going west towards St-Germain-des-Prés from the Latin Quarter, rue St-André-des-Arts is popular with young people and tourists enjoying the

Architectural detail at the Sorbonne

incessant animation around the cafés, crêperies, snack bars, souvenir shops and bookshops.

Cour du Commerce St-André, on the left, is an 18th-century arcade lined with shops and cafés embellished with picturesque old beams.
Métro: St-Michel.

La Sorbonne

This was the first and most successful of the many colleges that flourished in pre-revolutionary Paris. From very humble beginnings in 1253, it developed into a reputed centre of theological studies and became the seat of the powerful university. Its prestige and popularity have survived to this day. The 17th-century buildings were extensively remodelled and enlarged at the end of the 19th century. The Sorbonne church, which is open only on special occasions, dates from the beginning of the 17th century. It contains the white-marble tomb of Cardinal Richelieu.
Rue de la Sorbonne, 75005: for information on a free guided tour call 01 40 46 22 11. Métro: Cluny-La Sorbonne.

Walk: Quartier Latin

This is the centre of university life, where restaurants and cafés along and around the boulevard St-Michel are invariably packed. This beautiful area is perfect for a walk at all hours: during the day for visiting the shops and museums; at night to try one of the traditional restaurants; or over the weekend, to enjoy to the full the relaxed atmosphere.

Allow 2 hours (excluding a visit to the Musée National du Moyen Âge).

Start from the place St-Michel, with its impressive 1860 fountain. Take rue de la Huchette, rue de la Harpe and rue St-Séverin to reach the church of St-Séverin (see p59).

1 St-Séverin Quarter

The narrow streets and alleyways have kept their picturesque medieval names, such as 'rue de la Parcheminerie' (Parchment Street). Unfortunately, the authenticity of the district is threatened by the increasing number of cheap Greek and North African restaurants, with a welcome exception: La Cochonaille. Le Caveau de la Huchette (rue de la Huchette) is a well-known jazz cellar. *Go round the back of St-Séverin, down rue St-Jacques to the church of St-Julien-le-Pauvre. Then follow rue Galande and rue Lagrange to place Maubert.*

2 Place Maubert

Maubert is probably a contraction of Maître Albert, the famous 13th-century teacher. At one time the hideout of thieves and cut-throats, the area has been renovated and has regained its atmosphere. The tiny rue Maître Albert leads down to the river, from where you get a beautiful view of Notre-Dame. *Turn right on quai de Montebello and right again. Rue de Bièvre brings you back to place Maubert.*

3 St-Nicolas-du-Chardonnet

This unusual 17th-century church with a 20th-century façade is decorated inside with paintings by Corot and Le Brun, and elaborate funeral monuments. *Proceed away from place Maubert and along rue du Sommerard to the Musée National du Moyen Âge (see pp52–3). Walk up rue de la Sorbonne and rue Victor Cousin, then left into rue Soufflot.*

4 Place du Panthéon

Facing you is the vast domed Panthéon (*see pp53–4*), which dominates the Latin Quarter. Sit at one of the cafés and admire the view before continuing past the Bibliothèque Ste-Geneviève –

famous for its ancient manuscripts – and the highly original church of St-Étienne-du-Mont (*see p58*).
Turn right into rue Clotilde, then left into rue de l'Estrapade.

5 Place de la Contrescarpe

This tiny square has been famous since the Middle Ages for its *cabaret de la Pomme de Pin* (at No 1), described by the famous author François Rabelais.
Following rue Lacépède to the end, you will arrive at the Fontaine Cuvier (see p51). Turn left into rue Monge.

6 Arènes de Lutèce

Rue des Arènes, on the right, leads to the ruins of a Roman theatre discovered during the remodelling of medieval Paris in the 19th century, and now part of a public garden.
Turn left at the crossroads into rue du Cardinal Lemoine, right into rue Clovis, right into rue Descartes, then continue down rue de l'École Polytechnique.

7 Collège de France

Since its foundation by François I in 1530 the college has maintained a tradition of independent teaching, and still gives free public lectures.
Continue along rue des Écoles. Cross boulevard St-Michel into rue l'École de Médecine.

8 Rue Hautefeuille

This old, picturesque street on your right takes you back to place St-André-des-Arts (*see* rue St-André-des-Arts, *p55*).

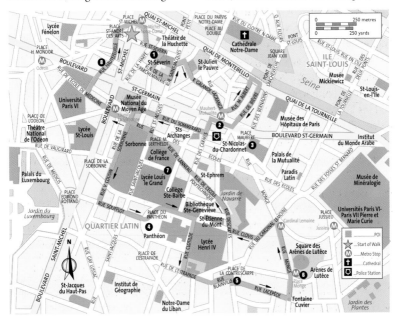

The striking façade of St-Étienne-du-Mont

St-Étienne-du-Mont

Begun in 1492, the church was only completed in 1626. Its originality lies in its harmonious combination of styles: the chancel and the tower are late Gothic, and the Renaissance façade is unique with its three superimposed pediments. Inside, the church is well lit by a row of windows replacing the traditional triforium. The magnificent rood screen, framed by two graceful open spiral staircases, was built at the beginning of the 16th century by Antoine Beaucorps according to drawings by Philibert Delorme. Notice the beautiful pulpit, dating from 1650, and the attractive 16th-century stained glass behind it. Past the rood screen on the right is St Geneviève's shrine, containing relics of the patron saint of Paris. Philosopher and mathematician Pascal and the playwright Racine are buried behind the chancel.

1 Place Ste-Geneviève, 75005, behind the Panthéon. Open: Tue–Fri 8.45am–7.30pm, Sat 8.45am–12.45pm & 2–7.45pm, Sun 8.45am–12.15pm & 2.30–7.45pm, Mon noon–7.30pm. Métro: Cardinal-Lemoine.

St-Julien-le-Pauvre

There has been a church on this site since the 6th century, as it was on the route followed by pilgrims on their way to Santiago de Compostela. The present building, which dates from the late 12th century, was the university church from the 13th to the 16th century. St-Julien is now a Greek Orthodox church. Its style is transitional, partly Romanesque and partly Gothic, with a 17th-century façade. *St-Julien-le-Pauvre, rue St-Julien, 75005. Métro: St-Michel.*

St-Médard

This late Gothic church was completed in the 17th century. Inside there is a 16th-century triptych, as well as other paintings of the French school and an interesting 17th-century organ loft.

LITERARY CAFÉS

Several cafés near the church of St-Germain-des-Prés have been the rendezvous of intellectuals and artists. Le Procope, rue de l'Ancienne Comédie, just off Carrefour de l'Odéon, is the oldest. It was opened in 1686 by a Sicilian whose excellent coffee drew actors from the Comédie-Française opposite. Later it attracted philosophers including Voltaire and Rousseau, revolutionaries such as Danton, Robespierre and Marat, and the famous 19th-century writers and poets Musset, George Sand, Balzac and Hugo. The claim to fame of Le Flore and Les Deux Magots is far more recent. In the late 1940s and 1950s they became the haunt of Sartre, Simone de Beauvoir, Camus, Prévert and the post-war generation of philosophers and poets. They are still favoured by today's intellectuals, but the magic has gone.

Rue Mouffetard, 75005. Closed: Mon.
Métro: Censier-Daubenton.

St-Séverin

Situated in one of the oldest districts
of Paris, St-Séverin is named after a
hermit who lived in the area in the 6th
century. Work on the present building
began in the 13th century, and went on
until 1530. Thus, the façade and part of
the nave are basically early Gothic,
while the rest is late Gothic.

In 1681 the Grande Mademoiselle,
Louis XIV's cousin, had the chancel
altered by the famous architect
Le Brun. The 13th-century west door
originally belonged to a nearby church
that was demolished in 1839. Inside, the
most remarkable feature is the double
ambulatory, with its spiral central
columns looking like palm trees under
the ribbed vaulting. There is beautiful
16th-century stained glass in the upper
windows, and modern stained glass by
Bazaine in the chapels at the east end.
Rue des Prêtres St-Séverin, 75005.
Open: Mon–Sat 11am–7.30pm, Sun
9am–10.30pm. Métro: St-Michel or
Cluny-La Sorbonne.

Jardin des Plantes

Founded in 1626, the botanical gardens
were greatly extended by the famous
18th-century naturalist Buffon, and the
menagerie was created during the
Revolution. The **Musée d'Histoire
Naturelle** (Museum of Natural
History) houses departments of
botany, mineralogy, palaeontology

The timeless beauty of St-Séverin

and entomology. The gardens include:
the **Jardin Alpin (Alpine Garden)**
with 2,000 species of plants from
mountainous regions from the Alps
to the Himalayas; the **Jardin d'Hiver
(Winter Garden)**, housing heavy-
scented tropical plants and flowers;
a number of hothouses; a maze;
and a herb garden devoted to
medicinal plants.
Entrance from rue Cuvier, rue Buffon
and Place Valhubert, 75005.
Tel: 01 40 79 56 01. www.mnhn.fr.
Gardens, menagerie, museum and
maze open daily 7.30am–7.45pm.
Admission charge for the museum.
Métro: Jussieu, Gare d'Austerlitz.

ST-GERMAIN-DES-PRÉS

Situated on the left bank, in the Latin
Quarter, St-Germain-des-Prés has, since

the days of Sartre and the Existentialists, been known as the rallying place of the intellectual avant-garde, who traditionally met in the literary cafés of the boulevard St-Germain. The district nestles round the ancient church of St-Germain-des-Prés and abounds in interesting contrasts.

The wide boulevard St-Germain, cutting right across it and carrying fast traffic eastwards, spoils the immediate surroundings of the church a bit, but the backstreets are delightful, each having its own attractive feature. There is rue de Buci with its lively open-air market, and the very old streets in the vicinity of the quaint place de Furstenberg – rue Cardinale, rue de l'Échaudé, going back to the 14th century, and rue Bourbon-le-Château.

Further west rue Bonaparte and rue des Saints-Pères, running down to the river, are lined with old-fashioned

Place St-Germain-des-Prés with its church

antique shops and art galleries, while rue Jacob, at right angles to them, is one of the most pleasant streets in the area. On the busy boulevard St-Germain, near place St-Germain-des-Prés, are the well-known cafés closely associated with the district – Les Deux Magots and Le Flore.
Métro: St-Germain-des-Prés or Mabillon.

Place St-Sulpice

Dominated by its monumental fountain and the twin-towered church of St-Sulpice, this square is an ideal place for a pause while visiting St-Germain-des-Prés.
Métro: St-Sulpice or Mabillon.

Fontaine des Quatre Points Cardinaux

Standing in the centre of the charming place St-Sulpice, this fountain is the work of the architect Visconti. Facing the four cardinal points of the compass are the busts of four well-known men of the church who never became cardinals.
Place St-Sulpice, 75006. Métro: St-Sulpice, Mabillon.

St-Sulpice

The church was originally built by the Abbey of St-Germain-des-Prés as a parish church for the surrounding area. The present building was started in 1646, and many architects worked on it until 1732, when it was decided to abandon the austere classical style. The Florentine architect, Servandoni, was selected to give the church an Italian-style façade.

Notice two giant shells mounted on supports carved by Pigalle as you enter; they were offered by the Venetian Republic in 1745. The first chapel on the right as you face the chancel has remarkable murals full of romantic inspiration, painted by Delacroix between 1849 and 1861.
Place St-Sulpice, 75006, near the Luxembourg gardens and St-Germain-des-Prés. Open: daily 7.30am–7.30pm. Métro: St-Sulpice.

St-Germain-des-Prés

This was the church of a powerful Benedictine abbey, a great centre of learning, which owned most of the Left Bank until the 17th century. The abbey buildings were destroyed during the 1789 Revolution, but the Romanesque church was saved and restored in the 19th century. It offers an original mixture of styles: the chancel and nave are Romanesque with Gothic vaulting, the massive tower acquired a steeple in the 19th century, and the original porch is masked by a door added in 1607. Inside, the chancel and ambulatory are the most interesting parts: notice the traditional carvings on the capitals and the ornamental triforium; the marble shafts of its columns come from the original 6th-century church.
Place St-Germain-des-Prés, 75006. Open: Mon–Sat 8am–7.45pm, Sun 9am–8pm. Métro: St-Germain-des-Prés.

The historic centre

Walk: St-Germain-des-Prés

Literary cafés, jazz cellars, informal bistros, bookshops, fashion boutiques and antique shops, as well as one of the oldest churches in Paris, are the main attractions here. Get lost in the maze of small streets that make the area around Saint-Germain so charming. If you are not in the mood to shop, sit at one of the cafés and people watch enjoying the beauty of Paris and its people.

Allow 2 hours.

Start from the Odéon métro station.

1 Carrefour de l'Odéon

Cross over the boulevard St-Germain: No 130 marks the entrance of the Cour du Commerce St-André. This alleyway and covered arcade has revolutionary associations: Marat's newspaper, *L'Ami du Peuple*, was printed at No 8, and it was here that Dr Guillotin's deadly invention was first tested on sheep. *Retrace your steps and turn right.*

2 Rue de l'Ancienne Comédie

The most prestigious theatre company in France, the Comédie-Française, performed at No 14 until 1770. The Café Procope opposite has, since 1686, been the meeting place of writers, politicians and philosophers. *Follow rue de l'Ancienne Comédie to the embankment, and turn left.*

3 Institut de France

The 17th-century domed building by Le Vau houses the Bibliothèque

Mazarin, including Cardinal Mazarin's own collection of rare books. Since 1805 it has also housed the Institut de France, founded during the 1789

Relaxing by a floral forest

Revolution. It includes the Académie Française, set up by Richelieu in 1635. *Turn left into rue Bonaparte; on the right is the École des Beaux Arts (Academy of Fine Arts). Turn left into rue des Beaux Arts.*

4 Rues des Beaux Arts, Seine, Visconti and Jacob

This whole area has had many famous inhabitants including Oscar Wilde, Racine, Balzac, Delacroix and Corot. Rue de Seine is lined with art galleries, and rue Jacob has many antique shops and several quiet hotels.
From rue Jacob turn right into rue de Furstenberg.

5 Place de Furstenberg

This charming little square is lined with romantic catalpa trees and old-fashioned street lamps. Delacroix had his studio at No 6; this is now a national museum with mementoes of the artist.
Open: Wed–Mon 9.30am–5pm.
Closed: Tue.
Rue de l'Abbaye brings you back to rue Bonaparte; turn left. The church of St-Germain-des-Prés, once part of a powerful abbey, is on your left.

6 Place St-Germain-des-Prés

Immediately on your right is the café Les Deux Magots and, almost next door, Café de Flore, where intellectuals and artists have been meeting for generations. It is a good spot to get the feel of the area over a cup of coffee. The Brasserie

Lipp opposite is a rather more select rendezvous for celebrities.
Continue up rue Bonaparte, then turn left into rue St-Sulpice. Pass the church and turn right along rue de Tournon.

7 Luxembourg

Marie de' Medici, widow of Henri IV, had the palace modelled on the Palazzo Pitti in Florence. It is now the seat of the Sénat. The gardens are adorned with numerous statues and the famous Fontaine de Médicis (*see p52*).
Coming out of the gardens, follow rue Rotrou to place de l'Odéon. Rue Crébillon and rue Condé take you back to Carrefour de l'Odéon.

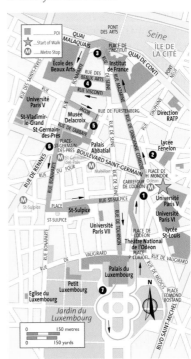

North and west of the historic centre

The grandeur of Paris is definitely visible in the neighbourhoods to the north and west of the historic centre. Mainly developed under Napoleon, the areas around Invalides, the Palais Royal and the Champs-Élysées epitomise France's glorious side. Montmartre may be the exception to this, but from its vantage position it is the perfect place to admire Paris.

PLACE DE L'ÉTOILE
Arc de Triomphe

The Arc de Triomphe has, like the Tour Eiffel, a magnetic appeal for visitors from all over the world. This can, to a large extent, be explained by its exceptional situation at the top of a hill, almost halfway between the Louvre and La Défense. Its square outline, easily spotted from afar, is well defined against the sky by day and illuminated by night.

GLORIOUS AND SOMBRE MOMENTS

In 1885 Victor Hugo, France's most popular man of letters, lay in state beneath the arch before being buried in the Panthéon.

On 14 July 1919 the allied armies celebrated victory by marching through the arch.

In 1940 the German army marched past it, greeted only by deadly silence.

In 1944 General de Gaulle was given a riotous welcome.

On 14 July 1989 the arch was the focal point of the joyous national celebrations for the bicentenary of the 1789 Revolution.

Commissioned in 1806 by Napoleon as a tribute to his Grande Armée, it is the largest triumphal arch ever built in the pure tradition of Roman architecture. The design was that of architect Jean Chalgrin. However, work progressed slowly (it took two years to lay the foundations!). Chalgrin died in 1811, and the construction of the arch almost came to a halt after the fall of Napoleon. It was finally completed in 1836.

In 1840 the hearse carrying Napoleon's remains passed, quite appropriately, under the arch on its way to the Invalides. Then, in 1920, the Unknown Soldier was buried beneath it, under a plain slab, and, since 11 November 1923, a remembrance ceremony has been held every year. The flame is rekindled every evening at 6.30pm. On special occasions a huge flag floats beneath the arch to splendid effect.

The arch is 50m (164ft) high, 45m (148ft) wide, and 22m (72ft) thick. Of the four sculptures on the façades,

(*Cont. on p68*)

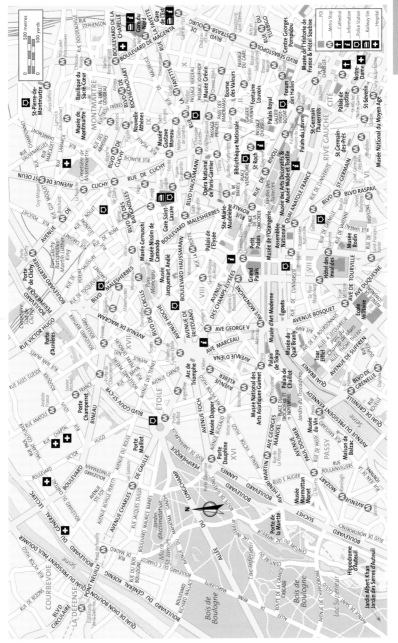

Walk: The Champs-Élysées

The name is French for 'Elysian Fields', the place of the blessed dead in Greek mythology. The sense one gets while walking along this avenue is truly that of grandiosity. The Champs-Élysées is lined by expensive outlets, which make this strip of land one of the most famous shopping streets in the world. This symbol of French elegance and glamour offers a unique and thrilling view that sweeps uphill to the Arc de Triomphe.

Allow 2 hours.

Start from place de la Concorde (métro Concorde).

1 Champs-Élysées

The avenue was designed in the 17th century as a royal way leading out of Paris towards Versailles. Later it became extremely fashionable to be seen driving along it in a horse-drawn carriage. In recent years the Champs-Élysées has been the scene of all major national celebrations, such as the bicentenary of the 1789 Revolution.
Start walking along the main avenue.

2 Concorde to the Rond-Point

The paved avenue is lined with green open spaces planted with chestnut trees after the English fashion. The romantic alleys lead to half-concealed pavilions, such as those occupied by the American Embassy and the Espace Cardin.
Walk through the gardens on the left, and turn right along the Cours La Reine, then right again into avenue Winston Churchill.

3 Petit Palais

Like the Grand Palais facing it, the Petit Palais was built of stone and steel for the 1900 Exposition Universelle, and now houses the art collections of the city of Paris: Greek, Roman and Egyptian art; medieval and Renaissance objects, books and enamels; 16th- and 17th-century Dutch and Flemish paintings; 18th-century furniture and tapestries; and 19th-century French paintings by masters such as Delacroix and Cézanne.
Tel: 01 53 43 40 00.
www.petitpalais.paris.fr

4 Grand Palais

In this imposing, glass-roofed building, adorned with an Ionic colonnade and elaborate sculptures, major art exhibitions are traditionally held.
At the back is the **Palais de la Découverte**, a science museum that is great for children.
3 av. du Général Eisenhower. Tel: 01 44 13 17 17. www.grandpalais.fr. Open: Thur–Mon 8am–10pm, Tue 9.30am–

*10pm, Wed 10am–10pm. Cross the
Champs-Élysées and continue along
avenue de Marigny.*

5 Palais de l'Élysée

The Palais de l'Élysée, built in 1718,
counts among its famous owners the
Marquise de Pompadour and Napoleon's
sister Caroline. Since 1873 it has been the
official residence of the president.
*Turn left into rue du Faubourg
St-Honoré, lined with shops, then left
again into avenue Matignon.*

6 Rond-Point des Champs-Élysées

Designed by the 17th-century
landscape architect Le Nôtre, most
famous for his work on the gardens of

Versailles it has an array of beautiful
flowerbeds and fountains, and several
of the surrounding buildings date from
the 19th century.
Continue up the Champs-Élysées.

7 Rond-Point to the Arc de Triomphe

Of the fashionable mansions built
around 1860, only one has survived,
No 25. It belonged to La Païva, an
adventuress whose receptions were
attended by writers and artists.
Today the wide pavements teem
with a cosmopolitan crowd. On the
quieter, south side is Fouquet's
Restaurant, where celebrities come
to be seen.

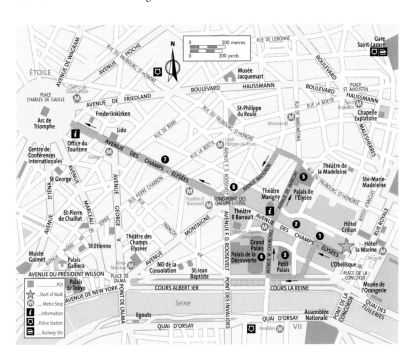

only the one by François Rude is famous. Known as La Marseillaise, it depicts the departure in 1792 of the volunteers, spurred on by a winged figure representing France.

Smaller reliefs on the façades and the sides feature victories won during the 1789 Revolution and the First Empire; a frieze by Rude and five other sculptors runs all round the arch. Along the top runs a row of shields inscribed with the names of victories won by Napoleon's Grande Armée.

A subway leads from the northern pavement of the Champs-Élysées to the base of the arch. Underneath, the names of hundreds of generals are inscribed on the walls: those who died in action are underlined. It is worth heading to the platform on top of the arch by means of the lift or stairs. The perfectly symmetrical place de l'Étoile and the 12 avenues radiating from it offer a stunning view. To the west is the vast modern complex of La Défense. The small museum houses an exhibition explaining the construction of the arch, as well as the main events connected with it; there is also a video show in French and English. *http://arc-de-triomphe.monuments-nationaux.fr*

Place de l'Étoile, where the arch sits, is so called because of its star shape. It was renamed place Charles de Gaulle, after the World War II general; but here tradition dies hard and 'l'Étoile' it

The Arc de Triomphe floodlit at night

remains in the hearts of all Parisians even now.

Over 150 years ago Haussmann remodelled it and built elegant neo-classical mansions all around. The 120m (394ft)-wide avenue Foch is the most exclusive residential street in Paris; among its past illustrious inhabitants were the Duke and Duchess of Windsor.
Tel: 01 55 37 73 77. Open: daily 10am–11pm (winter 10am–10.30pm). Admission charge. Métro: Charles de Gaulle-Étoile. Access by subway from the north side of the Champs-Élysées.

Around Arc de Triomphe
Parc Monceau
Situated in a fashionable residential area, close to the Arc de Triomphe, the Parc Monceau was landscaped as an English garden, with rocks and an oddly shaped lake, and adorned with mock ruins, pyramids and statues following the neoclassical style fashionable in the 18th century.
Boulevard de Courcelles. Métro: Monceau.

Égouts (Sewers)
The sewers formed part of the modernisation programme that was undertaken by Baron Haussmann in the 19th century, with the network totalling some 2,000km (1,250 miles). The visit includes the showing of a video film that explains how the whole system works.
Place de la Résistance, 75007. Tel: 01 53 68 27 81. Open: Sat–Wed 11am–4pm (5pm in summer). Closed: Thur–Fri. Admission charge. Métro: Alma-Marceau.

Musée Nissim de Camondo
This private mansion backing on to the Parc Monceau was donated to the nation by the Comte de Camondo. It re-creates the interior of an elegant 18th-century house with furniture made by the most famous cabinetmakers, and with Beauvais tapestries, precious ornaments and china.
63 rue Monceau, 75008. Tel: 01 53 89 06 50. Open: Wed–Sun 10am–5.30pm. Closed: Mon–Tue. Admission charge. Métro: Villiers or Monceau.

Musée Cernuschi
The house and personal collection of oriental art of banker Henri Cernuschi form the basis of this museum, bequeathed to the city of Paris before his death in 1896. Ancient Chinese art, including Neolithic terracottas, is particularly well represented.
7 avenue Vélasquez, 75008. Tel: 01 53 96 21 50. Open: Tue–Sun 10am–6pm. Closed: Mon. Admission charge. Métro: Monceau or Villiers.

TOUR EIFFEL AND TROCADÉRO
Its spindly greyish figure has been painted, photographed, joked about, written and sung about more than any other monument in Paris, and today, after more than 120 years, the Tour Eiffel still retains the key to its initial success: instant appeal. Once your curiosity is roused, it will continue to

Once vilified on aesthetic grounds, the Tour Eiffel is now a favourite subject of artists

'France will be the only nation with a 300m flagstaff!'

The tower was completed by 300 workers in just over two years from January 1887 to March 1889. This was made possible by the extreme precision of the plans, which gave the exact measurements for over 12,000 metallic parts. Two-and-a-half-million rivets were used and, when it was inaugurated, it was the tallest building in the world.

The tower's success was immediate. During the six months of the exhibition nearly two million visitors came to see the 'iron lady', and by the end of the year three-quarters of the building cost had already been recovered. The tower may have had its fans, but it also had its critics. Three hundred writers and artists signed a protest addressed to the municipality, qualifying it as 'useless and monstrous'.

Concession had been granted to keep the structure standing for 20 years only, and the tower was due to be pulled down in 1909.

However, by then it was playing an essential role in the rapidly developing

grow as you get closer and you will never be disappointed, for it is a strange monument indeed, with its graceful outline combined with the huge steel struts that are locked together in an intricate web.

Tour Eiffel (Eiffel Tower)

It is no surprise that the idea for such a daring project should have come from a group of engineers, headed by Gustave Eiffel, working on steel bridges and viaducts. Plans submitted by Maurice Koechlin and Emile Nouguier won first prize in a competition organised for the 1889 World Exhibition, and Gustave Eiffel exclaimed enthusiastically:

VITAL STATISTICS

Total height: 320m (1,050ft). First floor: 57m (187ft). Second floor: 115m (377ft). Third floor: 276m (906ft). 1,710 steps to the top. Weight: 7,000 tonnes. Maximum sway at the top: 12cm (4³/₄in). Forty tonnes of paint are needed to repaint it every seven years. It has seven million visitors a year.

world of telecommunications. It was saved, and proved to be an indispensable asset in establishing the first radio telephone service across the Atlantic, and as a meteorological station. In 1957 its height increased by another 20m (66ft) when a television transmitter was fitted at the top. In preparation for its hundredth anniversary it was given a new look and completely repainted, and glitters elegantly now under more powerful lights.

A visit to the viewing platforms is a must. The view from the top floor is breathtaking, and can extend as far as 67km (42 miles) in exceptional weather conditions. If you wait until late afternoon on a clear day, the sun has had time to disperse all signs of morning mist. You will almost certainly have to queue for the lifts, as the tower is very popular. On your way up you may wish to stop on the first floor where there is a free video show on the history of the building.
Champ de Mars, 75007.
Tel: 01 44 11 23 23. www.tour-eiffel.fr.
Open: daily 9.30am–11pm (9am–midnight in summer). Admission charge.
Métro: Trocadéro or Bir-Hakeim.
RER: Champ de Mars-Tour Eiffel.

Trocadéro
Musée Marmottan Monet
This museum has, as a result of various bequests, developed from the original private collection into a museum of Impressionist painting. It bears the

name of the art historian Paul Marmottan who, in 1932, donated his house and private collections to the Académie des Beaux Arts. These included Renaissance tapestries, furniture and sculpture, as well as early 19th-century paintings and various objets d'art.

Following other legacies, the museum acquired some beautiful medieval manuscripts and its first Impressionist paintings, including Monet's famous *Impression: Sunrise* (1872), which gave the movement its name.

However, the outstanding asset of the museum is the collection of 65 paintings by Monet donated by his son in 1971. Exhibited in a specially built underground gallery, they testify to Monet's love of his country home in Giverny (*see p139*).
2 rue Louis Boilly, 75016. Tel: 01 44 96 50 33. www.marmottan.com.
Open: Tue–Sun 11am–6pm.
Closed: Mon. Admission charge.
Métro: La Muette.

Musée National des Arts Asiatiques Guimet
Founded in the 19th century by Émile Guimet, the recently renovated museum houses a major collection of Far Eastern art. Exhibits are from Cambodia, Vietnam, Burma, Nepal, Tibet and China. On the second floor there are some beautiful Chinese ceramics.
6 place d'Iéna, 75016. Tel: 01 56 52 53 00. www.museeguimet.fr.

Ships' figureheads at the Musée de la Marine

Open: Wed–Mon 10am–6pm.
Closed: Tue. Admission charge.
Métro: Iéna.

Musée du Quai Branly

The Musée du Quai Branly is devoted to the arts and populations of Africa, Asia, Oceania and the Americas.
37 quai Branly. Tel: 01 56 61 70 00.
www.quaibranly.fr. Open: Tue–Wed &
Sun 11am–7pm, Thur–Sat 11am–9pm.
Closed: Mon. RER: Champ de Mars-
Tour Eiffel.

Palais de Chaillot

This site has been much sought-after for its superb views of the river, the Tour Eiffel and the Left Bank.

Catherine de' Medici had a country house built on the Chaillot hill. In 1937 the present building was erected for the World Exhibition. Twin pavilions with curved wings are separated by a vast terrace. The palace houses the Théâtre National de Chaillot, one of the leading French theatres (*www.theatre-chaillot.fr*), and three museums: the Cité de l'Architecture et du Patrimoine, the Musée de l'Homme and the Musée de la Marine (*see below*).
Place du Trocadéro, 75016.
Métro: Trocadéro.

Cité de l'Architecture et du Patrimoine

This collection is a dizzying ensemble of sculpture, frescoes and portals from French churches and châteaux – all of it copies and casts. The effect is fascinating and hypnotic: saints and sinners, demons and angels, animals and mythical creatures compete for attention. Upstairs galleries give an overview of modern and contemporary architecture with a real apartment designed by Le Corbusier in 1952.
Tel: 01 58 51 52 00. www.citechaillot.fr.
Open: Wed & Fri–Mon 11am–7pm,
Thur 11am–9pm. Closed: Tue.
Admission charge.

Musée de la Marine Founded in 1827 by Charles X, this museum illustrates all kinds of maritime transport from battleships to pleasure boats with the help of scale models and actual crafts. There is an interesting royal toy called

Louis XV, Marie-Antoinette's pleasure boat at Versailles, a rowing boat specially built for Napoleon in 1811, and the *Belle Poule* in which his remains were brought back to France from the island of St Helena. The *Gloire*, dating from 1859, was the first armoured warship in the world. And, of course, exhibits include ships used for exploration, such as the *Astrolabe*, which took Dumont d'Urville to the Antarctic in the 19th century, and mementoes of the great explorers La Pérouse, Brazza and Charcot. Temporary exhibitions are a regular feature. *Tel: 01 53 65 69 69. www.musee-marine.fr. Open: Wed–Mon 10am–6pm. Closed: Tue. Admission charge.*

Palais de Tokyo

Situated just upriver from the Palais de Chaillot, the Palais de Tokyo was also built for the 1937 World Exhibition in much the same style. It houses the Musée d'Art Moderne de la Ville de Paris (*see below*) and a contemporary arts centre. The surrounding terraces feature statues by Emile Bourdelle. *13 avenue du Président Wilson, 75016. www.palaisdetokyo.com. Métro: Alma-Marceau.*

Musée d'Art Moderne de la Ville de Paris
The museum is housed in the east wing of the Palais de Tokyo. *La Fée Électricité*, painted by Dufy for the 1937 World Exhibition in Paris, is exhibited in the museum alongside other works of 20th- and 21st-century art. *Palais de Tokyo, 75016.*

Tel: 01 53 67 40 00. www.mam.paris.fr. Open: Tue–Sun 10am–6pm. Closed: Mon.

16th *arrondissement*
Passy
Annexed to the city of Paris in 1860, the 'village' of Passy is today a much sought-after residential district in the western part of the capital.

Maison de Balzac This museum is devoted to the 19th-century novelist who depicted French society with such mastery. It contains manuscripts,

(*Cont. on p76*)

A series of pools fronts the Palais de Chaillot, across the river from the Tour Eiffel

North and west of the historic centre

Walk: From Trocadéro to the Invalides

This is the Paris of grand vistas and wide-open spaces, where various architectural styles help to create an impressive setting for the most famous of the city's monuments, the Tour Eiffel.

Allow 2 to 3 hours (excluding museum visits and a climb to the top of the Tour Eiffel).

Begin from the Trocadéro métro station.

1 Place du Trocadéro

From the top of the Chaillot hill, the rather dull place du Trocadéro offers stunning views of the left bank. Behind a high wall to the west is the Cimetière de Passy and, facing the river, the Palais de Chaillot, built for the 1937 Exposition Universelle. The name Trocadéro commemorates the capture in 1823 of Fort Trocadéro in Spain.
Pass between the curved wings of the Palais de Chaillot.

2 Jardin du Trocadéro

Stairs lead down to the gardens on either side of a long pool adorned with stone and gilt-bronze statues and attractive floodlit fountains, which provide the most spectacular summer night shows.
Cross the Pont d'Iéna, named to commemorate Napoleon's victory over the Prussians in 1806. Enjoy a good close-up view of the Tour Eiffel.

3 Parc du Champ de Mars

The vast open space, stretching from the Tour Eiffel to École Militaire, was originally designed in the 18th century as a parade ground for the nearby military academy, hence its name. It is often now used for large-scale public festivals and World Exhibitions; in 1989 almost half a million people attended the mammoth celebrations for the 100th birthday of the Tour Eiffel.
Walk across the park and turn right into avenue de la Motte-Picquet.

4 École Militaire

The building of this magnificent neoclassical military academy, designed by Louis XV's architect, Jacques-Ange Gabriel, was actually financed by a special tax on playing cards. Napoleon Bonaparte was undoubtedly its most famous cadet, passing out as a lieutenant in the artillery with the comment: 'Will go far, given favourable circumstances'. The school is still used as an instruction centre and is closed to the public.

As you walk round the building you might enjoy a short detour to the antique shops of the Village Suisse across the avenue de Suffren.

5 UNESCO Building

Inaugurated in 1958, this building is the result of three international architects – Hungarian-American Marcel Breuer, an Italian and a Frenchman – working together on the project, while the decoration was left to famous artists: Henry Moore (monumental sculpture), Alexander Calder (mobile), Pablo Picasso (mural), Joan Miró (ceramics), Lurçat and Le Corbusier (tapestries) and Isamu Noguchi (fountain).
Follow avenue de Lowendal and walk to No 51 bis, boulevard de la Tour Maubourg.

6 Musée de L'Ordre de la Libération

The Order of the Liberation, created by General de Gaulle in 1940, is the highest honour bestowed by France in recognition of outstanding services rendered during World War II. Among the allied leaders honoured are King George VI, Winston Churchill and General Eisenhower.
Tel: 01 47 05 04 10. www. ordredelaliberation.fr. Open: daily 10am–5pm (until 6pm summer). Closed: first Monday of the month. Retrace your steps and turn left. Go through the Hôtel des Invalides (see pp112–13), and walk across the Esplanade to the Invalides métro station.

Walk: From Trocadéro to the Invalides

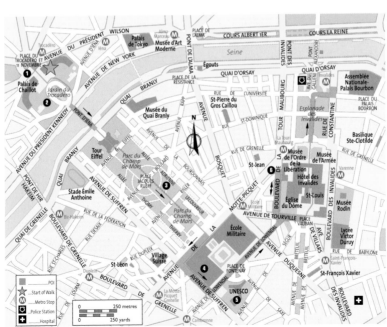

caricatures and engravings. Balzac lived here for seven years and regularly evaded his creditors by slipping out through the back entrance in the cobbled rue Berton.
47 rue Raynouard, 75016. Tel: 01 55 74 41 80. Open: Tue–Sun 10am–6pm. Closed: Mon. Admission charge. Métro: Passy. RER: Kennedy Radio France.

Musée du Vin The museum has found an apt home in the ancient cellars of the 15th-century former Passy Monastery; wine tasting is included in the visit.
Rue des Eaux, 75016. Tel: 01 45 25 63 26. www.museeduvinparis.com. Open: Tue–Sun 10am–6pm. Closed: Mon. Admission charge. Métro: Passy.

Jardin des Serres d'Auteuil
Plants used for decorating public buildings and for official occasions are grown in greenhouses here.

The huge tropical house contains palm trees, banana trees and a host of tropical plants. Rare species are also housed in a number of hothouses.
3 avenue de la Porte d'Auteuil, 75016. Open: daily 10am–5pm (winter); 10am–6pm (summer). Admission charge. Métro: Porte d'Auteuil.

Jardin Albert Khan
Situated just south of the Bois de Boulogne, this succession of gardens, created by the banker Albert Khan, illustrates landscapes from different regions of the world: the forest of

Vosges, a Japanese garden, an English garden, as well as a picturesque rock setting. The display of hundreds of flowers is at its best in late spring.
14 rue du Port, 92100 Boulogne. Open: daily 11am–6pm. Admission charge. Métro: Pont-de-St-Cloud, then bus No 72, 52 or 175.

Musée Dapper
The first museum in Paris dedicated entirely to Africa – ancient and modern – displays excellent wooden statues and masks, bronzes, historical paintings and prints, as well as receptacles, textiles

The exquisitely beautiful interior of Galerie Vivienne

and jewellery. The wood-panelled hall is a fine setting for lively displays of music, dance and theatre.
35 rue Paul Valéry, 75116.
Tel: 01 45 00 91 75. www.dapper.fr.
Open: 11am–7pm. Closed: Tue between exhibitions. Admission charge. Métro: Victor Hugo.

GRANDS BOULEVARDS

The Grands Boulevards on the right bank, slicing through the heart of the capital between the place de l'Opéra and the place de la Bastille, make you feel the real pace of Parisian life. Having replaced obsolete fortifications at the end of the 17th century, the boulevards became a popular place for strolling. However, a marked difference soon developed between east and west, the latter being the fashionable end.

Today, it is still fascinating to notice the change as you walk east from the Opéra. Just off the boulevard des Italiens on the right is the Opéra Comique, specialising in light opera. In the boulevard Montmartre on the left is the Musée Grévin, the famous waxworks, while on either side of the boulevard are two 19th-century shopping arcades.

Further east, two 17th-century monumental gates mark the entrance to the boulevard St-Denis and the boulevard St-Martin. South of the boulevard de Bonne Nouvelle is a rather seedy district called Le Sentier, a centre of the wholesale trade in fabrics and ready-made clothes.

Arcades

Covered arcades were in fashion at the end of the 18th century and at the beginning of the 19th. Some of them, like Galerie Vivienne (*see p83*), were elaborately decorated. Called *galeries* or *passages*, they are today lined with boutiques. The best are between rue de Rivoli and the Grands Boulevards, west of boulevard de Sébastopol. The following should not be missed:
Galerie Vivienne *4 place des Petits-Champs, 75002. Métro: Bourse.*
Passage Choiseul *44 rue des Petits-Champs, 75002. Métro: Quatre Septembre.*
Passage des Princes *97 rue de Richelieu, 75002. Métro: Richelieu-Drouot.*
Passage des Panoramas *11 boulevard Montmartre, 75009. Métro: Grands Boulevards.*
Passage Jouffroy *10 boulevard Montmartre, 75009. Métro: Grands Boulevards.*
Passage Verdeau *31 bis rue du Faubourg-Montmartre, 75009. Métro: Le Pelletier.*
Passage du Caire *2 place du Caire, 75002. Métro: Sentier.*
Galerie Vérot-Dodat *19 rue Jean-Jacques Rousseau, 75001. Métro: Palais-Royal.*

Bibliothèque Nationale (National Library)

Under French law publishers are required to submit copies of all works they publish, as well as computerised
(*Cont. on p80*)

Baron Haussmann's revolution

Just over 150 years ago a revolution shook Paris to its very foundations and altered the city more drastically than even 1789 had done. It was orchestrated by one man, Baron Haussmann, with the enthusiastic approval of Napoleon III. By 1850 the town had grown around its medieval centre without any coherence, and the squalid, narrow streets were a constant health hazard. Moreover, growing social problems threatened the fragile political stability.

From 1853 to 1870 Haussmann's engineers and architects cut right through the heart of the old city, laying waste whole districts, installing an adequate water supply and a network of sewers, creating wide avenues and building rows and rows of six-storey blocks of flats, which have become one of the familiar sights of the town.

Modern Paris emerged out of the chaos and soon became known as *la ville lumière*, a harmonious ensemble of green open spaces including the Bois de Boulogne, of spacious, tree-lined boulevards and imposing public buildings such as the Opéra.

Haussmann's far-seeing town planning was conceived on a scale that left room for expansion, and by the end of the century the railway

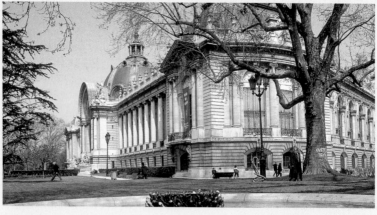

Georges Eugène Haussmann, town planner extraordinaire, whose vision created modern Paris – with buildings such as the Petit Palais ...

... and the Opéra Garnier

stations, the Tour Eiffel, and the Grand and Petit Palais had all taken their rightful places on the Paris scene.

The painful surgery Haussmann imposed on the capital was, however, much criticised at the time by such public figures as Victor Hugo, George Sand and Alexandre Dumas, who denounced the ruthless break with the past, and the crippling cost of these 'extravagant' schemes that encouraged speculation. Today Parisians have mixed feelings about the drastic transformation that Haussmann imposed upon the city. Many feel that the extreme orderliness of his style is more representative of an authoritative state than of Paris's true creative heart. Here and there, across different parts of the city, one can find entire streets designed as an explicit rejection of the Paris of Baron Haussmann. One great example is Rue Reaumur: in the 1890s, when the street was developed, a competition to design a new façade was declared. The competition was intended to encourage a new architectural style to counteract the visual sterility of Haussmann's avenues. But history has passed a more favourable judgement, for it was Haussmann who enabled Paris to blossom into the unique capital city it is today.

The elegant home of Musée Jacquemart André

and multimedia documents, at the Bibliothèque Nationale. To help house this exhaustive collection, another site was opened in 1996 at quai François Mitterrand in the 13th *arrondissement*. *58 rue de Richelieu, 75002. Tel: 01 53 79 59 59. www.bnf.fr. Open: Tue–Sat 10am–7pm, Sun 1–7pm. Closed: Mon & 1st–3rd week Sept. Métro: Bourse, Palais-Royal.*

Fontaine Louvois

This ornamental fountain by Visconti is a typical example of the decorative style used in urban architecture during the 19th century. The statues represent four French rivers: the Seine, Loire, Saône and Garonne.
Square Louvois, 75002, near the Bibliothèque Nationale. Métro: Bourse.

Musée Grévin

This waxworks, founded in 1882, provides good entertainment for the whole family. There are vivid historical scenes, and numerous life-size wax figures of famous people, as well as distorting mirrors.
10 boulevard Montmartre, 75009. Tel: 01 47 70 85 05. www.grevin.com. Open: Mon–Fri 10am–6.30pm, Sat–Sun 10am–7pm. Admission charge. Métro: Grands Boulevards.

Musée Jacquemart André

Situated right in the centre of town, but a little off the visitor's beaten track, this elegant 1870 mansion houses fine collections of Renaissance and 18th-century art, displayed in beautiful surroundings. They include portraits by Gainsborough and Reynolds, paintings and drawings by Rubens, Rembrandt, Van Dyck, Frans Hals and Ruysdael, 16th-century enamels and ceramics, some beautiful furniture, Beauvais tapestries and paintings by Boucher and Watteau.
158 boulevard Haussmann, 75008. Tel: 01 45 62 11 59. www.musee-jacquemart-andre.com. Open: daily 10am–6pm. Admission charge. Métro: St-Philippe-du-Roule or Miromesnil.

Opéra National de Paris-Garnier

The architecture of this ornately decorated and recently renovated opera house epitomises the elaborate style of the 1860s. It was designed by Charles Garnier, a young and then unknown architect, who was chosen because of the boldness of his plans, which departed from the usual neoclassical style. When the Opéra was inaugurated in 1875 its vast stage, able to accommodate nearly 500 artists, ranked it among the world's finest opera houses.

Groups of statues by various artists welcome visitors at the top of the steps at the main entrance. One of them, *La Danse* by Carpeaux, was considered highly risqué when it was created and has been replaced by a copy. The original is in the Musée d'Orsay.

The auditorium, which seats about 2,000, has red and gold as the dominant colours. The ceiling was painted by Chagall during the 1960s. The huge chandelier hanging in the centre weighs nearly 7 tonnes.

Place de l'Opéra, 75002.
Tel: 01 71 25 24 23.
Open: daily 10am–5pm, except during matinées and special events. Guided tours are available. Métro: Opéra.

Rue Royale

This elegant street, which links the place de la Concorde and the Madeleine, has wide pavements lined with luxury shops.

Near the place de la Concorde, Maxim's is still one of the leading restaurants of the capital.

Métro: Concorde or Madeleine.

North and west of the historic centre

The classical façade of La Madeleine, at the back, as viewed from place de la Concorde

Walk: From Opéra Garnier to Palais Royal

The prestigious Opéra Garnier and the elegant Palais Royal epitomise the impression of refinement and grandeur that one gets from this walk.

Allow 2 hours.

Begin from the place de l'Opéra (métro Opéra). Cross boulevard des Capucines, then turn right.

1 Rue de la Paix

Named rue Napoléon when it was opened in 1806, it is today lined with expensive jewellers (the famous Cartier is at No 13) and has become the symbol of luxury. It leads into the elegant place Vendôme, which Napoleon admires from the top of the central column.

Cross the square, walk along rue de Castiglione and turn left.

2 Rue St-Honoré

Le Carré des Feuillants is a fashionable but expensive restaurant where you can experiment with *la nouvelle cuisine*. Église St-Roch halfway down the street stood on a hillock known as Butte St-Roch, which was completely levelled for the building of avenue de l'Opéra: before that, you had to go down seven steps to gain access to the church; now you have to go up 13.

Further along the street, on the right, rue des Pyramides leads to the square that bears the same name, with a gilded statue of Joan of Arc, erected in the 19th century on the very spot where she was wounded while attempting to deliver Paris from English occupation.

Follow rue St-Honoré, which leads to the Palais Royal.

3 Palais Royal

As you reach the place André Malraux you get a splendid view of the Opéra to your left. Across the square is the Théâtre Français, home of the famous Comédie-Française (*see p40*). Close by is place Colette, from where you enter the Palais Royal gardens. Before you do, however, carry on a little further to the Louvre des Antiquaires, which has 250 shops and a convenient restaurant.

Walk through the Jardin du Palais Royal. Turn right into rue des Petits-Champs.

4 Galeries Colbert and Vivienne

These charming covered arcades date from the early 19th century; Galerie Vivienne is the most beautiful of the two, with its carved, vaulted ceiling and glass roof, and old-fashioned bookshop.
Rue des Petits-Champs leads to the circular place des Victoires with a statue of Louis XIV in the centre (see p43).
Leave by rue Vide-Gousset.

5 Notre-Dame-des-Victoires

The 17th-century church is famous for its paintings, its monument to Lully, and the 30,000 ex-votos on its walls.
Continue along rue Notre-Dame-des-Victoires, turn left past Palais de la Bourse (the Stock Exchange), then left again into rue de Richelieu.

6 Bibliothèque Nationale (National Library)

Since 1720 this has been the site of the Bibliothèque Nationale (originally Bibliothèque Imperiale), France's national library *(see pp77 & 80).*
Continue along rue Richelieu, turning right into rue Thérèse.

7 Fontaine Molière

Located at the corner of rue Molière and rue Richelieu, this fountain was built by architect Visconti in celebration of the French theatrical tradition and in particular Molière *(see p36).*
Turn right along rue Ste-Anne to rue des Petits-Champs. Go left, then walk back along avenue de l'Opéra.

Walk: From Opéra Garnier to Palais Royal

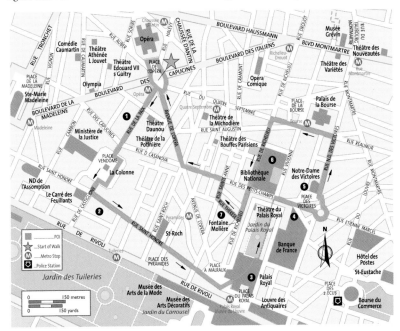

Ste-Marie-Madeleine

This church in the guise of a Greek temple is known to Parisians simply as La Madeleine. Two partly erected churches were successively razed before Napoleon had this temple built in honour of his Grande Armée. It was completed only in 1842, and by then it had been decided that the temple would be a church.

Fifty-two massive Corinthian columns surround the building, which dominates the centre of the place de la Madeleine with its flower market and well-known luxury delicatessens, Hédiard and Fauchon. Inside the church are some interesting 19th-century sculptures, including *Le Baptême du Christ* by François Rude and *Le Mariage de la Vierge* by Pradier. *Place de la Madeleine, 75008. Tel: 01 44 51 69 00. www.eglise-lamadeleine.com. Open: daily 9.30am–7pm. Métro: Madeleine.*

MONTMARTRE

The distinctive white outline of the Sacré-Cœur basilica, visible from almost anywhere in the city, is the universally recognised symbol of Montmartre. The name Montmartre draws on people's imaginations to keep alive the memory of its heyday. For, unlike other districts, La Butte relies entirely on its past image for survival. Quite often it looks like a vast open-air theatre where the décor never changes and the same play is enacted every day.

TOULOUSE-LAUTREC

Born into the aristocracy and crippled at an early age, Toulouse-Lautrec led a sad life made endurable by his talent and passion for painting. He portrayed scenes of Montmartre's nightlife, sketching its stars with unique realism.

The case of Montmartre is unique, for it was its picturesque rural atmosphere and its 'free and easy' life that caught the world's attention at a time when most cities were overwhelmed with industrial squalor. It had nothing to offer except its refreshing simplicity, and its artists.

It all began in the early 19th century, when a few artists and writers wishing to lead a freer life settled on the Butte: Berlioz, Nerval and Heine were three of the earliest residents. After the Franco-Prussian war of 1870 Montmartre became the centre of Paris's bohemian life, inhabited by impoverished painters and poets and visited by Parisians who flocked into the cabarets, cafés and dance halls.

At the turn of the 20th century the most famous of these establishments were the Chat Noir and the Moulin Rouge at the foot of the hill, the Moulin de la Galette halfway up in rue Lepic, La Bonne Franquette at the corner of rue des Saules and rue St-Rustique and the Lapin Agile down on the other side of the hill. Artists such as Renoir, Van Gogh and Toulouse-Lautrec found their inspiration among the enthusiastic spectators and the colourful performers. They were succeeded by Utrillo, Picasso, Braque, Modigliani and many others. This lasted until World War I, when the artists left for Montparnasse.

The artists are back and a few cafés and cabarets full of memories remain, but the heritage is very difficult to preserve in a rapidly changing city with a growing tourist trade.

The most interesting parts of Montmartre are today centred around rue Lepic and its market, as well as place des Abbesses and the surrounding area. However, it is worth strolling along rue des Saules or in place du Tertre: do it early in the morning or out of season if you want to avoid the crowds.

Cimetière de Montmartre

Access to the cemetery is by a flight of stairs on the left of rue Caulaincourt, at the end of the bridge as you walk towards the boulevard de Clichy. Ask for a map at the entrance. Many famous artists and writers are buried here, among them the novelists Stendhal and Zola, the composer Berlioz, the poets Heine and Vigny, the painter Degas and, more recently, the film director François Truffaut.
Rue Caulaincourt. Métro: Abbesses or Lamarck-Caulaincourt.

Montmartre, still a village at heart

Walk: Montmartre

Nestled on the highest hill of the city, Montmartre (or the 'mountain of the martyr' in reference to Saint Denis) was only annexed to Paris in 1860, allowing it to retain its village-like atmosphere. Famous for its distinctive white Sacré Cœur basilica and its history of artists and cabarets, the real charm of the area can be experienced by wandering off the regular tourist track.

Allow 2 hours.

Begin from the Abbesses métro station (note: as this is the deepest métro station in Paris, it is advisable to take the lift to exit the station).

1 Place des Abbesses

A chapel stands on the site where it is thought Saint Denis was martyred in the 3rd century – and nearby rue Yvonne Le Tac is supposedly where he was beheaded.

Nothing, however, remains of the important abbey that once stood in Place des Abbesses, giving it its name. Notice the métro entrance with its glass-roofed, wrought-iron structure, originally designed by Hector Guimard at the turn of the 20th century. Across the street is the Art Nouveau Église-St-Jean-de-Montmartre from the same era.
Leave by rue des Abbesses and turn right into the twisting rue Ravignan.

2 Place Émile Goudeau

On this charming square is a reconstruction of the Bateau-Lavoir,
burnt down in 1970, where Picasso and friends such as Braque, Modigliani, Juan Gris and others made history (*see p90*).
Continue to the end of rue Ravignan. Turn right through Place Jean-Baptiste Clément and follow rue Norvins.

3 Place du Tertre

Now focused on the tourist trade, with its abundance of bustling cafés and artists, this old village square has lost its authenticity but you can imagine what it was like in the 1920s. The tiny place du Calvaire in the southwest corner offers exceptional views of the capital.
Leave place du Tertre past the old church of St-Pierre de Montmartre (see p93) and walk to the Sacré-Cœur Basilica.

4 Sacré-Cœur

If you don't mind crowds, you will enjoy the majesty of the place and the vast panorama in front (*see p92*).
Walk across rue du Mont-Cenis and along rue Cortot.

5 Musée de Montmartre

Halfway down rue Cortot is the Museum of Montmartre. Time permitting, stop in to learn more about Montmartre's colourful history.
Turn right into rue des Saules.

6 Rue des Saules

This is one of the most picturesque streets in Paris, running downhill from the Butte. On the right is the Montmartre vineyard and, on the other side of rue St-Vincent, the Lapin Agile cabaret, hardly changed since the days of Picasso and Vlaminck. In the Cimetière St-Vincent, opposite, you can see Utrillo's grave.
Walk along rue St-Vincent and turn left up some stairs to the Château des Brouillards, an 18th-century folly.

Beyond is avenue Junot; turn left, then right twice to end in rue Lepic.

7 Moulin de la Galette

The old mill on your right was once a famous dance hall painted by Renoir and Van Gogh. The latter lived with his brother Theo, an art dealer, further down the hill at No 54.
Follow the street as it curves left, then as it turns right downhill.

8 Café des Deux Moulins

It was in this neighbourhood café where the fictional characters from the film *Le Fabuleux Destin d'Amélie Poulain* worked. It is a nice place to have a coffee and watch the locals passing by.
Follow the street to the bottom of the hill. On the corner stands the Moulin Rouge.

Walk: Montmartre

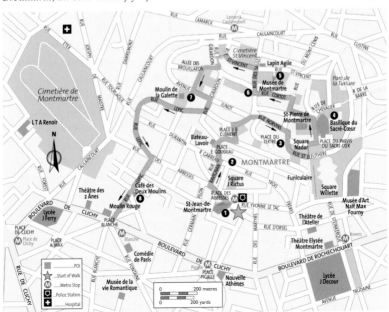

Fine artworks at the Musée Gustave Moreau

Musée de Montmartre

It is one of the oldest houses on the Butte, dating from the 17th century. The museum depicts the history of Montmartre through mementoes of its most famous inhabitants.
12 rue Cortot, 75018. Tel: 01 49 25 89 37. www.museedemontmartre.fr. Open: Tue–Sun 11am–6pm. Closed: Mon. Admission charge. Métro: Abbesses.

Nouvelle Athènes

South of the place Pigalle, this district owes its name ('New Athens') partly to the neoclassical architecture of its houses, and partly to the fact that, in the early 18th century, it attracted the artistic and intellectual elite of the capital, and rivalled Faubourg St-Germain.

Musée de la Vie Romantique

Housed in the former home of the painter Ary Scheffer, the museum is devoted to the artists, musicians and writers who used to be his regular guests: George Sand, Chopin, Delacroix, Liszt, Dickens, Turgenev and many others.
16 rue Chaptal, 75009. Tel: 01 55 31 95 67. Open: Tue–Sun 10am–6pm. Closed: Mon. Admission charge. Métro: St-Georges or Pigalle.

Musée Gustave Moreau

Another 19th-century painter's house that has been turned into a museum. Moreau's symbolism influenced his famous pupils at the École des Beaux-Arts – Rouault and Matisse.
14 rue de la Rochefoucauld, 75009. Tel: 01 48 74 38 50. www.musee-moreau.fr. Open: Wed–Mon, 10am–12.45pm & 2–5.15pm. Closed: Tue. Admission charge. Métro: Trinité or St-Georges.

Place Émile Goudeau

This unpretentious square, where the famous Bateau-Lavoir building (*see p90*) once stood, still possesses some of the old magic of Montmartre.
Métro: Abbesses.

The Sacré-Cœur basilica, today a city landmark

Capital of the arts

Ever since the 12th century, when students and tutors rejected the stifling teaching of the Church and moved to the left bank, Paris has been a centre of attraction for artists from all over the world, and the melting pot of new art movements. This long-standing tradition reached its climax during the second half of the 19th century.

It was after 1870 that Paris really became the world's artistic centre, being both a sanctuary for misunder-stood artists, such as Irish writer Oscar Wilde, and the birthplace of major art movements, such as Impressionism.

The 'Bateau-Lavoir' was the romantic name of a shabby wooden building in Montmartre, which at the turn of the 20th century housed poor artists including Modigliani, Van Dongen, Juan Gris and, above all, Picasso and Braque, who developed the Cubist style as a reaction against Impressionism. Picasso's *Les Demoiselles d'Avignon* was painted here. The artistic life is depicted in Puccini's opera *La Bohème*.

It was at that time too that Diaghilev created his Ballet Russe and that the premiere of Stravinsky's *Sacre du Printemps* caused a scandal at the Théâtre des Champs-Élysées.

The indecisive period between 1918 and 1939 was marked by the 'lost generation', a group of American writers including Ezra Pound and Ernest Hemingway, while the Exposition Internationale des Arts Décoratifs et Industriels in 1925 launched a new style, Art Deco.

After the difficult post-World War II period, Paris is now reclaiming its position as a leader in contemporary art. New galleries have opened in various parts of town, from the historically artsy Montmartre (*see pp84–93*) to the area around Les Halles, to the up-and-coming neighbourhoods in the east of the city. The clearest sign of this increasing interest in contemporary art is probably the recent opening of the prestigious Gagosian Gallery (*4 rue Ponthieu, 75008. Tel: 01 75 00 05 92. Métro: Franklin D Roosevelt*) – a new temple to contemporary art that covers 900 square metres across four levels. The inauguration of the Centre Pompidou has been followed by other major projects such as the Opéra Bastille and La Villette, which offer a new range of artistic experiences.

Original works of art can be found along the banks of the Seine

The Parisian art scene has also recently turned its spotlight on street art. Now there's no need to go into museums and galleries to see the hottest artists around. Ephemeral artworks by the likes of Jêrome Mesnager and Space Invader appear and disappear on the streets of Paris, before being taken down by the police or picked up by collectors. Keep your eyes peeled for these amazingly original graffiti, mosaics and stencil works.

The Paris Museum Pass enables you to visit some 60 buildings in the Paris region. It is on sale at participating museums and monuments or online at en.parismuseumpass.com, and is available for two days, four days, or six days. National museums are free the first Sunday of every month.

MODERN ART TRENDS

Fauvism: an early 20th-century trend characterised by a simplification of form and use of bright colours.

Cubism: an early 20th-century movement concerned with rendering form and volume through geometric shapes.

Abstract Art: a movement started in 1910 by Kandinsky and rejecting figurative representation of reality. Developed mainly from 1950 onwards, especially in the USA with Abstract Expressionism.

Surrealism: a 1920s trend that rejected all conventions and aimed at expressing the subconscious mind.

Realism and New Realism: from 1960 onwards these trends mark a return to figurative painting with the introduction of objects from everyday life.

Sacré-Cœur

Visible from almost anywhere in Paris, the white basilica has become one of the city's most famous landmarks. The decision to build it was taken by the Assemblée Nationale in 1873, to boost public morale after the Franco-Prussian War. Work started in 1875 but the building was only completed in 1914, and consecrated after World War I. The architecture is a bit disappointing, but its Byzantine basilica makes it highly visible on the skyline. The mosaic decorating the chancel vaulting is impressive. It is possible to go up to the top of the dome for a superb view of Paris.

Parvis du Sacré-Cœur, 75018.
Tel: 01 53 41 89 00.
www.sacre-coeur-montmartre.com.
Basilica open: daily 6am–10.30pm.
Dome and crypt open: 9.30am–7pm
(summer), 10am–6pm (winter).

The cavernous Grande Arche de la Défense has a rooftop exhibition gallery

Admission charge to crypt and dome.
Métro: Anvers, then access
by funicular.

St-Pierre-de-Montmartre

This is one of the oldest churches
in Paris, once part of the powerful
Abbey of Montmartre. Built in the
12th century, it has an 18th-century
façade. Inside there are some fine
carvings on the Romanesque
capitals, contrasting with the
modern stained glass, as well
as four marble columns probably
belonging to a Roman temple that
stood on the site.

ON THE OUTSKIRTS

The region around Paris is rich with
beautiful palaces, châteaux and modern
getaways that make for perfect day
trips. From the lavish Versailles to
historic Fontainebleau and the
entertaining Disneyland® Paris, all
visitors will find something that appeals
to them. Further afield, too, lie a
number of not-to-be-missed towns and
attractions. Chartres is the 'acropolis' of
medieval sculpture and architecture,
while Chantilly and Vaux-le-Vicomte
offer excellent cultural days out.

La Défense

This entirely modern district lies to the
west of Paris, across the Pont de
Neuilly. A statue in the central square,
symbolising the defence of Paris during
the Franco-Prussian war of 1871, gives
the area its name.

Town planners had been toying for a
long time with the idea of extending the
Voie Triomphale. This broad avenue,
designed by Le Nôtre in the 17th century,
sweeps across the city in a straight line
from the Louvre to the Arc de Triomphe.

Development began in the late 1950s,
and architects experimented with new
ideas. One of the driving principles was
the total separation of pedestrian and
motorised traffic. The vast complex is
surrounded by a *boulevard circulaire*
(ring road) carrying through-traffic,
with underground link roads and
outlets leading to specific areas at
different levels.

A broad pedestrian avenue, called the
Esplanade du Général de Gaulle, rises
in steps from the Seine and gives access
to the various groups of buildings: a
variety of towers housing offices, a few
blocks of flats, a vast shopping complex
called Les Quatre Temps, and the CNIT
(Centre National des Industries et des
Techniques), the oldest building on
the site. Its concrete shell, resting on
just three supports, was considered
revolutionary in 1958. It has recently
been converted into an international
business centre. Development of La
Défense continues today with the
designs of several renowned architects
represented in the skyline.

Inaugurated in 1989 just in time for
the bicentenary of the Revolution, La
Grande Arche was the last project to be
built. Designed by the Danish architect
Otto von Spreckelsen, the arch is shaped
like a huge hollow cube so vast that

The Orangerie at Parc de Bagatelle

Notre-Dame (spire included) would fit beneath it! It is faced with glass and white Carrara marble, and is slightly out of alignment with the axis of the Voie Triomphale. The complex glass-and-steel structure of the external lifts offsets the extreme simplicity of the outline, and the *nuages* (clouds) suspended below the arch add a whimsical touch. The lifts take visitors up to the roof (Le Belvédère) to admire the view.

Although the area is perfectly safe during the day, it is unfortunately not so at night and is best avoided out of working hours, especially the métro and RER station.

3.5km (2¼ miles) west of the Porte Maillot. Métro & RER (A): Grande Arche de la Défense.

Bois de Boulogne

This favourite haunt of nature-loving Parisians, covering about 850ha (2,100 acres), is crowded at weekends but offers peace and quiet to those who wander off the beaten track along its shady avenues (take care after dusk). Many family activities are available: boating on the lakes, cycling along specially designed lanes, horse riding and fishing. The **Jardin d'Acclimatation**, on the northern edge of the 'Bois', is a comprehensive amusement park for children, with rides, a train and a zoo; and there are clearly marked picnic areas.

This former royal hunting forest used to abound with deer, bear and wild boar until Louis XV opened it to the public and it became fashionable. Given to the city of Paris in 1852 by Napoleon III, it was remodelled into an English-style park by Baron Haussmann, who created lakes, ponds and the Longchamp racecourse. The Auteuil racecourse was built after the Franco-Prussian War in 1870, and at the turn of the 20th century fashionable horse-drawn carriages could be seen driving along the wide avenues that nowadays carry fast traffic bound for the *banlieue* (suburbs) just across the Seine.

In the northwest corner of the 'Bois' is the **Parc de Bagatelle**, a beautiful garden well known for its spring display of tulips and irises, and roses and water lilies in summer. The nearby **Jardins de Bagatelle** is an expensive restaurant in a lovely setting.

The **Pré Catelan**, in the centre of the Bois de Boulogne, is another attractive park with a magnificent 200-year-old copper beech; next to it the **Jardin Shakespeare**, planted with flowers and trees mentioned in Shakespeare's plays, has a charming open-air theatre.

Entry from the north side. Métro: Les Sablons, Porte Maillot. Bagatelle, métro: Pont-de-Neuilly then No 43 bus to place de Bagatelle. East side, RER: Avenue-Henri-Martin. South side, métro: Porte d'Auteuil. Bicycle rental available at the lakes; horse riding at the Société d'Equitation de Paris, route de la Muette à Neuilly. Tel: 01 45 01 20 06.

Bois de Vincennes

See p101.

East of the historic centre

Historically known as working-class Paris, the east side of the city is increasingly home to trendy artists and chic restaurants. Walk around Bastille to discover up-and-coming designers as well as some of the best markets Paris has to offer. Head to beautiful Père Lachaise for some peace, or go for a jog on the lovely Viaduc des Arts.

BASTILLE

Traditionally occupied by craftsmen and small shopkeepers, the district had, by the end of the 1970s, become generally rundown. Following complete renovation it shows every sign of becoming as chic and sought-after a place as its neighbour, the Marais. Art galleries, bars and fashionable nightclubs are to be found cheek by jowl with old-fashioned shops and dilapidated houses. The most colourful and liveliest streets are rue de la Roquette and rue de Lappe to the north of the square.

Built in the 14th century as part of new fortifications to extend the city on the right bank, the Bastille was also intended as a residence for Charles V, who felt safe here. During the reign of Louis XIII it became the hated state prison and symbol of oppression.

The Bastille held some famous prisoners, including the Man in the Iron Mask (allegedly Louis XIV's twin brother), the finance minister Fouquet and the philosopher Voltaire. Shortly before the Revolution the prison was partially cleared and held only seven prisoners when the mob took it by storm on 14 July 1789. However, its fall unleashed the spirit of freedom throughout France.

Demolition began soon after. Some of the stones were used for the construction of Pont de la Concorde, and within a year there was no trace of the massive fortress. On the first anniversary of the fall of the Bastille, people danced on the site.

Even though all traces of the gruesome past disappeared long ago, the name Bastille is still charged with significance. In the minds of French people it has remained a symbol of the fight for freedom, commemorated every year on 14 July.

Opéra Bastille

In 1989, the fate of the whole district took a different turn with the opening

(Cont. on p100)

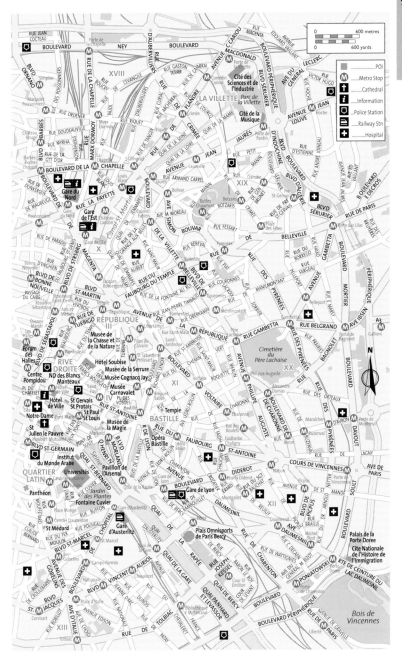

Revolutionary Paris

Ever since Paris was granted independent status in the 13th century Parisians have never hesitated to rise up against excessive political power, and the city has come to be considered as a very sensitive barometer of discontent.

The first major duel between the monarchy and the French people was fought and won in Paris in 1789. The signal was given when the crowd swept along Faubourg St-Antoine to bring down the mighty Bastille on 14 July (still celebrated as a national holiday today). As a symbolic gesture, Pont de la Concorde was later completed with stones from the hated prison so that 'the people could forever trample the ruins of the old fortress'. Time and again Parisians took the initiative, marching on Versailles to ask the king for bread, charging the Tuileries guards, listening to their leaders' fiery speeches in the Palais Royal gardens, watching with gruesome curiosity as the rickety carts

Place de la Concorde

Bastille Day is still a major holiday in France

full of condemned prisoners jolted along the streets to the place of execution, or simply dancing and rejoicing on Champ de Mars on the first anniversary of Bastille Day.

Scenes like these are vividly described in Dickens' *Tale of Two Cities*. King Louis XVI was executed by guillotine in place de la Concorde (then place de la Révolution) on 21 January 1793.

During the 19th century the streets of Paris were set ablaze on several occasions by fierce fighting across hurriedly erected barricades. With the 1848 uprising, which began in boulevard des Capucines, Paris did away with the monarchy for good. Yet in 1871 the Commune of Paris again challenged the government in a contest that ended in bloodshed in

the Père Lachaise cemetery. This time the Parisians lost.

A hundred years later they showed that tradition could easily be revived when, in May 1968, students and workers barricaded the streets, bringing about General de Gaulle's resignation.

Since nothing is left of the original Bastille, the visitor will have to look elsewhere to get a feel of Paris during the years of the revolution. A great spot to do so is the Musée Carnevalet, situated in the Marais. This museum, former palace of the Marquise de Sévigné, is dedicated to the history of Paris. Its collection of historical artefacts and paintings allows you to revisit and learn about items and events such as the guillotine, the storming of the Bastille and the women's march on Versailles.

Place de la Bastille: a bustling crossroads where a prison once stood

of Paris's second opera house, which had already become a controversial issue in various Parisian circles. It was intended to be technically more modern, and created a new artistic centre in the less favoured eastern part of Paris. Opéra Bastille, built by the young Canadian architect Carlos Ott, was inaugurated on 13 July 1989 as a preamble to the celebrations for the bicentenary of the French Revolution.

In stark contrast to the ornate Opéra Garnier, the gently curved, sober façade of the building catches the faintest ray of sunlight, thus brightening up the surrounding area.
Tel: 01 40 01 80 54 for guided tours.
www.operadeparis.fr.
Admission charge. Métro: Bastille.

Pavillon de l'Arsenal

Between place de la Bastille and the Seine is the Port de Plaisance de Paris Arsenal, a new marina. To the southwest, at the end of boulevard Henri IV, a museum, the Pavillon de l'Arsenal, illustrates architecture and town planning in Paris through the ages and new developments through changing temporary exhibitions.
21 boulevard Morland, 75004.
Tel: 01 42 76 33 97.
www.pavillon-arsenal.com.
Open: Tue–Sat 10.30am–6.30pm,
Sun 11am–7pm. Closed: Mon. Free
admission. Métro: Sully-Morland.

Place de la Bastille

The central column, called Colonne de Juillet (July Column), commemorates the Parisians who died during the July 1830 Revolution. This lasted only three days, *les Trois Glorieuses*; the victims were buried underneath the monument, and their names carved on the shaft. At the top of the 50m (164ft)-high column stands the elf-like figure of the *Génie de la Liberté*, the Spirit of Liberty. Paving stones follow the outline of the Bastille fortress on this otherwise ordinary square, which has become a traditional meeting place for demonstrations and celebrations.

VINCENNES

The Château and Bois de Vincennes lie just beyond the Périphérique, on the eastern side of Paris.

Situated on the edge of what was once a royal hunting ground, the recently restored Château de Vincennes dates from the 14th century. During the reign of Louis XIV, architect Le Vau built pavilions on either side of the courtyard. By then the keep had become a state prison, Fouquet and Mirabeau being among its unwilling guests. Extensive work has now restored the castle as it was in the 17th century.

Near the entrance, the Tour du Village, which formed part of the fortified wall, is the only one to have retained its original height of 42m (138ft). The imposing keep, 52m (171ft) high, is surrounded by a separate wall and moat. It houses a

The Royal Chapel in the grounds of Vincennes

museum depicting the castle's history. *Avenue de Paris, 94300 Vincennes. Tel: 01 48 08 31 20. www.château-vincennes.fr. Open: daily 10am–5pm (6pm in summer). Admission charge. Métro: Château de Vincennes.*

Bois de Vincennes

Generations of French schoolchildren know this as the place where Saint Louis used to administer justice seated under an oak tree. In 1860 Baron Haussmann remodelled it into an English-style park, with a racecourse. It is also home to a zoo and the **Parc Floral de Paris**, which hosts jazz and classical music concerts at weekends and in the summer. *Parc Floral de Paris, route de la Pyramide. Tel: 01 55 94 20 20. www.parcfloraldeparis.com. Open: daily 9.30am–5pm (winter); daily 9.30am–6pm (summer). Admission charge. Métro: Château de Vincennes. Parc zoologique – 53 avenue Daumesnil. Tel: 01 44 75 20 10. Open: daily 9am–6pm (6.30pm Sun). Admission charge. Métro: Porte Dorée.*

Bears in the zoo at the Bois de Vincennes

LA VILLETTE

The vast complex of La Villette has been developed on both sides of the canal de l'Ourcq, between the Porte de la Villette and the Porte de Pantin. Buildings on the original site have been incorporated into the project. The object of building a major new cultural centre on the edge of the city was to revive interest in this long-neglected eastern district, while taking advantage of the enormous amount of space that was available.

The Maison de la Villette

Housed in the recently renovated Rotonde des Vétérinaires, this section of the park puts on exhibitions of urban culture and history. The park extends across the canal de l'Ourcq: green open spaces, with red *folies* (follies) dotted about. These are see-through cubical pavilions, varying in shape and used for practical purposes. There is a children's centre, information centre, video studios, café and first-aid centre. The Grande Halle, dating from 1867, is an iron structure that was a cattle market until the 1970s. It is now a venue for exhibitions and trade fairs.

The **Zénith** is a vast hall that has the capacity to accommodate approximately 6,500 spectators and is used mainly for rock concerts.

La Géode

This shiny steel globe, close to the main building, acts as a vast mirror reflecting the surroundings and the changing sky with great intensity. The auditorium has a 1,000sq m (10,764sq ft) hemispheric screen. Films on scientific subjects are shown throughout the day. *www.lageode.fr. Film shows are every hour 10.30am–8.30pm. Admission charge.*

Explora

This permanent exhibition, staged on three levels and including tours, activities and workshops, illustrates four broad themes.

The **Earth and the Universe** deals with the exploration of the oceans, the geological history of the earth, movements of the continents, travel and experiments in space. The Planetarium aims to explain the complexity of the universe with programmes such as 'Life and Death of a Star' and 'Space Oasis'. **The Adventure of Life** deals with the human environment, man and the secrets of life. **Man and Matter** is concerned with man's control of energy and other resources, transport and economic trends. **Language and Communications** covers the world of sounds and images and various aspects of man's social behaviour.

The centre also includes a fully computerised multimedia library with special material available for children (*Médiathèque*), a cinema showing documentaries and fiction films to introduce viewers to the world of science (*Cinéma Louis-Lumière*), and two discovery areas for children aged

2 to 7 (*Cité des enfants*) and 5 to 12 years (*Inventorium*).

Cité des Sciences et de l'Industrie

Inaugurated in 1986, the complex has already proved very successful, attracting an increasing number of visitors of all ages. Much more than a museum, it is a constantly updated reference centre, keeping track of the rapid evolution of science and technology. Its novelty lies in the fact that visitors are encouraged to take part in various projects and demonstrations. This makes it a realistic and entertaining study centre, particularly suitable for children.

The building itself, incorporating a former 19th-century auction hall, was designed by Fainsilber, who used the reflection of light off the steel-and-glass structure to achieve futuristic effects. The glass reveals mechanisms usually kept hidden, as in the main escalators or the glasshouses on the south façade. *Parc de la Villette, 30 avenue Corentin-Cariou, 75019. Tel: 40 05 80 00. www.cite-sciences.fr.*
Open: Tue–Sat 9.30am–6pm, Sun 9.45am–7pm. Closed: Mon. Admission charge; headsets for audio tour of Explora *in English can be hired. Métro: Porte-de-la-Villette or Corentin-Cariou.*

Cité de la Musique

This is the other main complex in the park. The home of the Conservatoire National Supérieur de Musique, the higher national music academy, it houses a concert hall and the Musée de la Musique (Museum of Music). *221 avenue Jean Jaurès, 75019. Tel: 01 44 84 44 84. www.cite-musique.fr. Métro: Porte de Pantin. Musée de la Musique: Open: Tue–Sat noon–6pm, Sun 10am–6pm. Closed: Mon. Admission charge.*

OTHER SIGHTS
Along Canal St-Martin

Canal St-Martin was dug in the early 19th century to link Canal de l'Ourcq, running eastwards from La Villette, and the Seine. It winds its way across the eastern districts of Paris over a distance of 4.5km (2³/₄ miles) and joins the river just south of Bastille.

Futuristic design at La Villette

The most picturesque section lies between rue du Faubourg du Temple and rue Louis Blanc. The most relaxing way to enjoy the canal is to take a three-hour cruise from Musée d'Orsay to La Villette. (*See* Organised Tours, *p184.*) For those who prefer to walk beside the canal, the best way is to start either from place de la République (*métro: République*) or place de Stalingrad (*métro: Stalingrad or Jaurès*).

Palais de la Porte Dorée
Aquarium Tropical

This magnificent aquarium has a large collection of tropical fish and even a pit with crocodiles. It is especially popular with children of all ages – they love the display of electric fish!

A pedestrian bridge over the calm waters of Canal St-Martin

293 avenue Daumesnil, 75012. Tel: 01 53 59 58 60. www.aquarium-portedoree.fr. Open: Tue–Fri 10am–5.15pm, Sat–Sun 10am–7pm. Closed: Mon. Admission charge. Métro: Porte Dorée.

Cité Nationale de l'Histoire de l'Immigration (Immigration Museum)

This marvellous Art Deco building is sadly identified with the 'white man's burden' view of French history – its frescoes portray French colonialists as humanity's benefactors in places such as southeast Asia and northern and central Africa. Inaugurated for the 1931 colonial exhibition, it later housed the Musée des Colonies (Colonial Museum) before it was recast as a museum about immigration.
293 avenue Daumesnil, 75012. Tel: 01 46 29 22 00. www.sevrescitececeramiques.fr. Open: Tue–Fri 10am–5.30pm, Sat–Sun 10am–7pm. Closed: Mon. Admission charge. Metro: Porte Dorée.

Temple

This district south of the place de la République was named after the Knights Templars. In 1808 the site became an open-air second-hand clothes market known as the Carreau du Temple; the clothes were laid directly on the pavement. Today cheap clothes are sold in a covered market, but the site has retained its picturesque name.
Métro: Temple.

Cimetière du Père Lachaise

This is Paris's largest cemetery. A plan is available at the main entrance to help you locate the graves of the famous: Alfred de Musset was buried beneath a weeping willow; the tragic lovers Héloïse and Abélard (see p52) are buried here; so too are Oscar Wilde (in a suitably extravagant tomb) and Molière, Baron Haussmann, actress Sarah Bernhardt, and singers Edith Piaf and Jim Morrison of The Doors. The cemetery makes an intriguing and beautiful setting for a mid-afternoon stroll.
Main entrance from boulevard de Ménilmontant, 75020. Tel: 01 40 71 75 60. www.pere-lachaise.com. Open: daily 8.30am–6pm. Métro: Père Lachaise.

Parc des Buttes-Chaumont

One of the great urban public parks of Paris, the Buttes-Chaumont opened in 1867 and is one of the earliest examples of an urban renewal project. Situated in the 19th arrondissement, east of the centre, this park was designed by JC Adolphe Alphand under the direction of Baron Haussmann and Napoleon III and landscaped on hilly wasteland. Reclaiming the site of medieval gallows and a gypsum quarry, Alphand transformed the 25ha (62-acre) crescent-shaped mass into a picturesque masterwork. From the small temple, romantically set on the island in the middle of the lake, the view extends to the Butte Montmartre.
Métro: Buttes-Chaumont.

South of the historic centre

Amid the mostly residential streets and green, leafy spaces of southern Paris are dotted a few of the city's key monuments, including Hôtel des Invalides, the Musée d'Orsay and Montparnasse Cemetery. The south of Paris also represents the city's cultural core: from the fashionable Rive Gauche to the artistic hub of Montparnasse. Stroll along the river, browsing the second-hand bookstalls and taking in the striking views across to the other side as you go.

MONTPARNASSE

In the 18th century this area was a place of popular entertainment as bars, restaurants and cabarets, just outside the city boundaries, could serve tax-free wine. The tradition survived even after the district became part of Paris during the second half of the 19th century.

Just before World War I, artists and poets suddenly moved from Montmartre to this unknown left bank district, which soon came into the limelight, attracting painters and also composers such as Stravinsky and Satie, and, later, the 'lost generation' of American writers. The wine pavilion from the 1900 Exposition Universelle was transferred to passage de Dantzig by a patron of the arts for the benefit of needy artists; it was given the romantic name of 'La Ruche' (the beehive), and soon welcomed Modigliani, Zadkine, Chagall and Léger. Matisse, Picasso, Braque, Klee, Miró, Ernst, Cocteau and Apollinaire all lived in Montparnasse at

one time, their social life revolving round four cafés in boulevard Montparnasse: La Coupole, Le Sélect, La Rotonde and Le Dôme. Here they met with Russian political refugees such as Lenin and Trotsky.

Unlike Montmartre, this 'other' artists' stronghold was brutally drawn into the 20th century when a major town-planning project remodelled its centre during the 1960s and 1970s, but the old district is still centred around Carrefour Vavin, now place Pablo Picasso, where the well-known café-restaurants have survived. But whereas the décor has been carefully preserved, the establishments are certainly more upmarket now than in the days of Chagall. Just west of the Cimetière Montparnasse, rue de la Gaîté is, as its name implies, the centre of the district's nightlife. It is lined with cabarets, dance halls and theatres such as the Théâtre de la Gaîté-Montparnasse and the Théâtre Montparnasse.

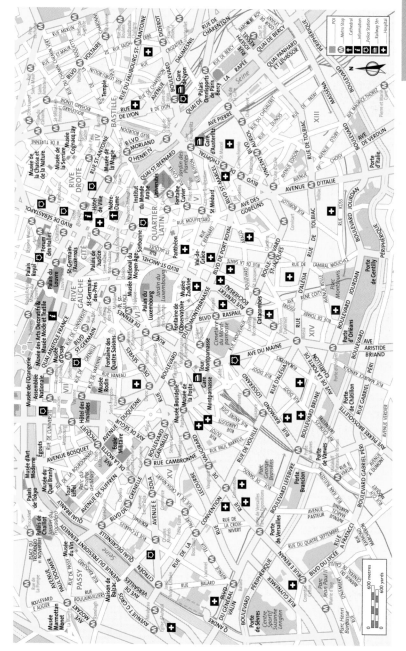

Ethnic Paris

Today foreigners account for one-sixth of the capital's population; thus, over the last few decades, the character of certain areas has drastically changed. Some minorities, such as the White Russians, are fully assimilated, even if they still get together on occasions. Others, however, live in enclaves that, over the years, have acquired a strong cultural identity.

The Jewish district is situated at the heart of the Marais, within a small quadrangle formed by rue de Rivoli, rue des Francs Bourgeois, rue Vieille-du-Temple and rue de Sévigné. There has been a Jewish community in this area since the Middle Ages, but the

Colonial connections, refugees and other immigrant groups are evident in the vibrant, cosmopolitan atmosphere of Paris's ethnic commercial ventures

arrival in 1962 of a great number of Algerian Jews suddenly altered the east European flavour of the district. Rue des Rosiers is very picturesque, with its delicatessens, restaurants, felafel snack bars and old food shops turned into fashion boutiques.

During the 1960s tower-block flats mushroomed in the 13th *arrondissement* and a large number of Asian immigrants, the majority of them Chinese, settled in the area surrounding porte de Choisy. As a result, avenue d'Ivry is particularly lively with its cinemas, restaurants, supermarkets, and shops that look like pagodas.

Successive waves of immigrants, this time mainly from Africa, have settled in the Goutte d'Or district, just east of Montmartre, and now more than 30 different nationalities cohabit in what must truthfully be called deteriorating conditions.

Redevelopment is in the air, understandably opposed by the locals, for what will become of the colourful little shops that do a roaring trade selling exotic groceries, junk jewellery and African fabrics?

In the summer of 2005 tensions reached a peak and France, Paris in particular, was shaken by a strong racial revolt. For weeks, people living in the outer neighbourhoods of Paris – many from the country's North

Ethnic influences add a splash of colour to Paris's largely uniform streets

African immigrant communities – set thousands of cars on fire and vandalised shops and schools, turning the streets of Paris's *banlieue* into war zones. As a result the French have been forced to deal with the changing face of their country, now home to Europe's largest Muslim population.

Unrest had partially abated since the protests of 2005, to be rekindled somewhat in 2010 when the senate voted in favour of a bill to ban face-covering veils in public.

Cimetière de Montparnasse (Montparnasse Cemetery)

The main entrance is in the boulevard Edgar Quinet. Many writers, artists and composers are buried here: among them the poet Baudelaire, the novelist Maupassant, the critic Sainte-Beuve, the philosopher Sartre and his lifelong companion Simone de Beauvoir, the composers César Franck and Saint-Saëns, and the sculptors Rude, Bourdelle and Zadkine. On the eastern edge of the cemetery *The Kiss* is an interesting sculpture by the Romanian artist Constantin Brancusi, who lived in Paris for many years.

Musée Bourdelle

The museum occupies the house and studio of Antoine Bourdelle, a disciple of Rodin, whose bust is among the exhibits. There are also some very interesting portraits of Beethoven.
16 rue Antoine Bourdelle. Tel: 01 49 54 73 73. Open: Tue–Sun 10am–6pm.

Closed: Mon. Admission charge. Métro: Montparnasse.

Musée de la Poste

The museum depicts the history of postal services, and has some fascinating exhibits such as the balloon used during the siege of Paris in 1870. There is also a collection of French stamps and a display of contemporary machines and methods.
34 boulevard de Vaugirard, 75015. Tel: 01 42 79 24 24. www.museedelaposte.fr. Open: Mon–Sat 10am–6pm. Closed: Sun. Admission charge. Métros: Montparnasse (exit place Bienvenue), Pasteur and Falguière.

Tour Montparnasse

At the heart of the new development stands the 200m (656ft)-high, 59-storey Tour Montparnasse. When it was built in the early 1970s it was Europe's tallest office block, and aroused fierce

Rue de la Gaîté: old theatres survive despite the street's changing character

controversy. The fastest of the 25 lifts climbs 6m (20ft) per second, reaching the top floor in 39 seconds. For most Parisians its only redeeming feature is the splendid panorama from the 56th and 59th floors. Across the pink-granite square in front of the tower is the new Gare Montparnasse.

33 avenue du Maine, 75015.
Tel: 01 45 38 52 56. Open: Mon–Fri
9.30am–11.30pm (10.30pm in winter);
Sat–Sun 9.30am–11pm.
Admission charge.

RIVE GAUCHE

This elegant district, bordering the Seine between the fashionable St-Germain-des-Prés and the stately Hôtel des Invalides, had its heyday in the 18th century. Two main thoroughfares, boulevard St-Germain and boulevard Raspail, cut across it, while the side streets, taken over by ministries, embassies and official residences, are wrapped in the kind of secluded atmosphere usually found in museums. Beautifully restored mansions of all sizes (some of them still privately owned) line the streets.

The general plan of the district is very neat, with the main *hôtels* (private residences) having been built along five parallel streets.

Nearer the river is rue de Lille with the Hôtel de Seignelay at No 80, now the Ministère du Commerce, and the Hôtel de Beauharnais, now the German ambassador's residence. Both were built in 1714.

Next comes rue de l'Université, so-called because the land once belonged to the university, with some of the earliest mansions: No 78, built in 1687, and No 51, dating from 1707.

The rue St-Dominique lost a few of its 18th-century houses when the boulevard St-Germain was opened.

In rue de Grenelle the most imposing mansion at No 110, dating from 1778, is now occupied by the Ministère de l'Éducation Nationale; the beautiful Fontaine des Quatre Saisons at Nos 57–59 (*see p112*) and the Hôtel Bouchardon next door epitomise 18th-century elegance and refinement. Hôtel Biron (Musée Rodin) and Hôtel Matignon (the office and home of the prime minister), at 77 and 57 rue de Varenne respectively, are probably the two most beautiful mansions of the whole district.

Assemblée Nationale (Palais Bourbon)

The seat of the lower house of the French Parliament (the Assemblée Nationale) consists of two 18th-century mansions: the Hôtel de Bourbon, which was originally built for one of Louis XIV's illegitimate daughters, the Duchess of Bourbon; and the Hôtel de Lassay. The two were joined in 1764 and a Greek-style façade was added in the 19th century to match that of the Madeleine. On the place du Palais Bourbon the original façade has kept its 18th-century appearance. To attend an Assemblée debate you must apply in writing.

33 bis quai d'Orsay, 75007. Tel: 01 40 63 77 77. www.assemblee-nationale.fr. Authorised group visits only on Saturdays. Métro: Assemblée Nationale.

Faubourg St-Germain

The name *faubourg* (suburb) is the only reminder of the area's suburban beginnings, when it was open countryside surrounding the Abbey of St-Germain-des-Prés. Around 1680 the aristocracy and the rich started to move in and, in the space of 50 years, the Faubourg had supplanted the Marais as the most fashionable residential district.

The imposing building of the Invalides

Fontaine des Quatre Saisons

This fountain was once the only means of water supply in the whole district. The street is too narrow to get a good view of this beautiful 18th-century fountain by Bouchardon. In the centre the city of Paris looks down on the rivers Seine and Marne, while on either side are figures representing the seasons.
57–59 rue de Grenelle, 75007. Métro: Rue du Bac.

Hôtel des Invalides

This imposing group of buildings, situated at the end of a vast oblong open space stretching across from the Seine, is an outstanding example of 17th-century classical architecture. Like Versailles, it epitomises the strength and confidence of the French monarchy under Louis XIV. Moreover, the whole surrounding area, with its wide, tree-lined avenues, the Faubourg St-Germain on one side and the Champ de Mars on the other, adds to the impression of space and grandeur. Sought-after by wealthy Parisians, it has become a quiet, secluded residential district.

At the beginning of his reign Louis XIV had difficulty in establishing himself on the throne of France, and realised the importance of a strong army. However, because of the appalling conditions faced by wounded soldiers, recruitment was difficult. In order to encourage potential recruits the king decided, in 1670, to found a hospital and pension home for 4,000 invalid ex-soldiers. Work started in 1671 and lasted for five years.

The king then commissioned the young architect Jules Hardouin-Mansart to design a church with a magnificent gilt dome. In 1840, after

years of negotiation with the British government, Napoleon's remains were returned to France and officially buried in the Église du Dôme, and the Invalides became a symbol of the Emperor's glory.

The best way to approach the Invalides is from the Pont Alexandre III (*see p115*). The vast Esplanade, designed by Robert de Cotte at the beginning of the 18th century, is 500m (550yd) long and 250m (275yd) wide. From here you can enjoy sweeping views of the harmonious ensemble of buildings. A formal garden, surrounded by a dry moat, has 17th- and 18th-century bronze heavy guns; beyond it, the impressive doorway, flanked by twin pavilions, is adorned with an equestrian statue of Louis XIV, dating from 1815.

Cour d'Honneur

The paved courtyard is lined with arcades on two storeys. Four pavilions have dormer windows adorned with trophies, and in the four corners, at roof level, there are carved horses trampling the emblems of war. More heavy guns complete this imposing setting. On either side of the courtyard are the collections of the **Musée de l'Armée** (*see p116*), while at the end is the entrance to Église St-Louis-des-Invalides.

Église du Dôme

The Église du Dôme was built between 1677 and 1735. The tiered façade with Doric and Corinthian columns is adorned with statues of St Louis, Charlemagne and the four virtues, and enhanced by the well-proportioned dome. The interior is magnificently decorated with different marbles, painted cupolas, columns and low reliefs. In the side chapels are the tombs of several of Napoleon's generals as well as those of Turenne, Lyautey and Foch. *Tel: 01 44 42 37 72. www.invalides.org. Open: Oct–Mar daily 10am–5pm, Apr–Sept daily 10am–6pm. Admission charge gives access to the church and five museums. Métro: Invalides or Varenne.*

The beautiful rococo Hôtel Biron, on boulevard des Invalides, houses the Musée Rodin

Bridges

Thirty-six bridges of greatly varying styles span the River Seine within Paris and are vital links between the left and right banks. Although some of them may have been rebuilt several times, their names often recall customs or events from various periods of the capital's history.

You can take them all in in a couple of hours and it will give you a unique perspective on Paris.

Passerelle Simone de Beauvoir

A pedestrian bridge opened in 2006 connecting the 12th and 13th *arrondissements* (the latter is the Paris Rive Gauche), formed by an undulating truss allowing two levels of decks that arrive at different levels each side of the river.

Pont au Double

This bridge acquired its strange name in the Middle Ages because the toll imposed at that time was a coin named a *double*.
Métro: St-Michel.

Petit Pont and Pont Notre-Dame

In Roman times these were the only bridges crossing the river via Île de la Cité. The Petit Pont, so-called because it is the smaller of the two, was first built of stone when the construction of Notre-Dame was undertaken, but periodic floods have taken their toll and it has been rebuilt 11 times. The present bridge dates from 1853. The Pont Notre-Dame, overladen with richly decorated houses, also had to be rebuilt several times. The present one dates from 1913.
Métro: St-Michel or Cité.

Pont au Change

Although built between 1858 and 1860, this bridge has a medieval name – a reminder that the houses and shops built on its predecessor belonged to moneychangers.
Métro: Châtelet.

Pont Neuf

Curiously enough, 'New' Bridge is the oldest bridge in Paris, dating from the 16th century. It was never built on, but the carvings that decorate it illustrate 'dentists' busily pulling teeth, entertainers and assorted stalls, all part of the daily scene 400 years ago. The two halves, which are not in line, are separated by place du Pont Neuf, where there is an

equestrian statue of King Henri IV.
Métro: Pont Neuf.

Pont des Arts

The city's first pedestrian iron bridge is a romantic structure dating from 1803.
Métro: Pont Neuf.

Pont Royal

This bridge epitomises the discreet elegance that is one of the most attractive features of Paris. It was built by Jacques Gabriel during the reign of Louis XIV – hence its royal name.
Métro: Rue du Bac.

Pont de la Concorde

Begun in 1788 by the civil engineer, Jean Rodolphe Perronnet, it was only completed after the fall of the Bastille. Since then it has reflected many political upheavals by changing its name every time something significant happens. In 1830 the name Concorde was adopted for good.
Métro: Assemblée Nationale.

Pont Alexandre III

Built for the 1900 Exposition Universelle, this bridge provides a link between the classical architecture of Les Invalides and the pompous steel-and-glass style of the Grand Palais. Each end is adorned with two allegorical sculptures, featuring medieval France and modern France on the left bank side, Renaissance France and France under Louis XIV on the right bank side.
Métro: Invalides.

Pont de l'Alma

The original Pont de l'Alma, built in 1854 to commemorate a Franco-British victory during the Crimean War, had to be replaced 20 years ago because the supports were sinking. However, the Zouave soldier beneath it, who indicates the level of the river, was preserved.
Métro: Alma-Marceau, Pont de L'Alma.

Pont Neuf, with its 12 varying arches

The Dôme church with its gilded cupola

Musée de l'Armée

This is one of the most comprehensive military museums in the world, with the collections housed in buildings around the main courtyard of Les Invalides.

On the west side is the **Galerie de l'Occident**. Among the exhibits in the ground-floor rooms is, remarkably, Henri II's suit of armour. The first floor is devoted to World War I and World War II.

On the east side is the **Galerie de l'Orient**. The ground floor has frescoes of Louis XIV's campaign in Flanders in 1672, and the famous paintings by Ingres of Napoleon's coronation. On the first floor there are mementoes of Napoleon. The second floor explores the Second Empire and the Franco-Prussian war of 1870. A recently opened wing is devoted to General de Gaulle and World War II.
Tel: 08 10 11 33 99.
www.invalides.org.

Open: daily Oct–Mar 10am–5pm; Apr–Sept 10am–6pm. Admission charge. Métro: Tour-Maubourg.

St-Louis-des-Invalides

This is the original church by Libéral Bruant, also known as the soldiers' church, a cold building decorated only with flags and standards taken from the enemy. The Église du Dôme is visible through a glass panel behind the altar. The magnificent organ was used for the premiere of Berlioz's *Requiem* in 1837.
Open: daily 10am–5pm, 6pm in summer. Métro: Varenne.

Musée d'Orsay

Ideally situated on the left bank, opposite the Jardin des Tuileries, this museum has taken its rightful place among the top European art museums. It is an unusual venue, housed in a converted railway station, which allowed the curators to depart from traditional display and to avoid monotony.

Inaugurated in 1900, the station was built on the site of Palais d'Orsay, which was burnt to the ground during the Commune of 1871. The architect,

NAPOLEON'S TOMB

In 1861 the architect Visconti designed a dramatic setting for the emperor's tomb. In the centre of an open crypt the red porphyry sarcophagus was placed on a base of green granite from the Vosges. Visitors can view it from the encircling balustrade within the Dôme.

Victor Laloux, was entrusted with the delicate task of designing a station that would not deface the surrounding area, in particular the Louvre and Jardin des Tuileries just across the river. He concealed the glass-roofed iron structure behind a beautiful stone façade, and adorned it inside with an elaborately decorated, coffered ceiling. However, less than 40 years later it had become obsolete, its platforms being too short for new electric trains.

In 1977 it was decided to convert the station into an art museum that would unite various collections covering the period from 1848 to 1914, including the famous Impressionist collection from the Jeu de Paume.

Thus, the new museum would make the link between the Louvre and the Musée National d'Art Moderne of the Pompidou Centre. It is an absolute must for anyone interested in 19th-century art.

When the museum opened in 1986 after a number of setbacks, it was universally acclaimed for the originality of its excellent interior design.

Les Invalides still houses some old veterans

The collections are exhibited in chronological order, on three main levels: the ground floor, the upper floor and the middle floor (in that order). In addition to the permanent collections, there are temporary exhibitions. Ground plans and leaflets in English are available near the entrance.

The ground floor

This floor is devoted to the period from 1848 to 1880. The sculpture section, in the central gallery, illustrates an interesting progression from the classical style of Pradier (*Sapho*) to the Romantic approach of Carpeaux, who carved the beautiful figures of the Fontaine de l'Observatoire (*see p122*). The rooms on the right and left of the gallery form the painting section. On the right, the classical trend is represented by Ingres (*La Source*), and the Romantic trend by Delacroix (*Chasse aux Lions*). Further on there

LES BOUQUINISTES

Second-hand bookstalls are one of the familiar sights of Paris, and a stroll along the river would be less enjoyable without them. The tattered, green-painted boxes that used to be carried to and fro by their owners have become permanent fixtures. At night they are locked, but in the afternoon they open one by one, like stranded sea shells, revealing books, prints, postcards and maps. A browse under their precariously propped-up lids is always fun, although there are not many rare editions or bargains to be found in them any more.

are some fine Puvis de Chavannes and early Degas. The rooms on the left show the progression from realism, with Daumier, Millet (*Les Glaneuses*), Courbet (*L'Atelier*) and the Barbizon school headed by Corot, towards Impressionism, represented by works painted before 1870: among them the famous *Déjeuner sur l'Herbe* by Manet and *La Pie* and *Femmes au Jardin* by Monet. In the architecture section there is an interesting model of the Opéra Garnier and its district.

The upper floor

Entirely devoted to Impressionism from 1872 and Post-Impressionism in a splendid festival of light and colour, the upper floor boasts works by Monet, Renoir, Sisley and Degas. Van Gogh, too, influenced by the movement, has his rightful place here; so does Cézanne, who stands apart as a pioneer of 20th-century painting.

Post-Impressionism is represented by Seurat, Toulouse-Lautrec, Henri Rousseau and his own naive style, Gauguin and the school of Pont-Aven, Bonnard, Vuillard, and so on.

The middle floor

This section is devoted to Naturalism and Symbolism, which became officially recognised themes at a time when Impressionism was rejected. It also contains works by early 20th-century artists such as Matisse and Bonnard.

LES QUAIS

The embankments are the city's main thoroughfares, carrying fast-moving traffic from east to west and vice versa. Lined with wide pavements planted with trees, they offer lovely walks along the river with fine views of the monuments situated on both banks of the Seine and on Île de la Cité.

On the right bank, quai de la Mégisserie and quai de Gesvres are lined with picturesque pet shops. From here there is a splendid view of the Conciergerie on Île de la Cité. The tiny square de l'Ave Maria offers an interesting view of the medieval Hôtel de Sens. Across the Pont Marie is Île St-Louis.

On the left bank there are striking views of Notre-Dame from quai de la Tournelle and quai de Montebello; just off the latter is the delightful square René Viviani. Past place St-Michel, quai des Grands-Augustins, named after a nearby monastery, is lined with second-hand bookstalls on the riverside, and has several 17th-century mansions on the other side. Pont Neuf, the oldest bridge in Paris, is in two sections, joining the right and left banks to Île de la Cité.

Musée Rodin

The superb collection of Rodin's sculptures is exhibited in the Hôtel Biron, where he lived from 1907 until his death in 1917. Some of his works, in bronze and white marble, are in the house, while others are distributed round the beautiful garden. A visit on a sunny day is highly recommended. In the garden are two of his most famous works – *Le Penseur* and *Les Bourgeois de Calais* – as well as *La Porte de l'Enfer* and *Ugolin*. On the ground floor there are more masterpieces, such as *Le Baiser* and *La Cathédrale*. On the first floor are the plaster casts used for the statues of Balzac and Victor Hugo.

77 rue de Varenne, 75007.
Tel: 01 44 18 61 10. www.musee-rodin.fr.
Open: Tue–Sun 10am–5.45pm. Closed: Mon. Admission charge. Métro: Varenne.

The sculpture gallery presents works by Rodin and his successors. The Art Nouveau section is well headed by Gallé, Lalique and Guimard.

1 rue de la Légion d'Honneur, 75007.
Tel: 01 40 49 48 14.
www.musee-orsay.fr.
Open: Fri–Sun & Tue–Wed 9.30am–6pm, Thur 9.30am–9.45pm. Closed: Mon. Admission charge. Facilities include: ground floor – bookshop, post office, bureau de change; upper level – coffee shop; intermediate level – restaurant. Métro: Solférino.

The Musée d'Orsay houses a superlative art collection, including Manet's *Olympia*

Walk: Rive Droite, Rive Gauche

This takes you from the 'royal' Jardin des Tuileries across the river to Faubourg St-Germain, once fashionable with the aristocracy, whose splendid mansions have now been taken over by ministries and embassies.

Allow 2 hours (excluding a visit to Musée d'Orsay).

Begin from the Concorde métro station.

1 Rue de Rivoli

The elegant arcades, once lined with smart boutiques, now house souvenir shops. The Hôtel Meurice, at No 228, served as headquarters of the German high command during World War II.
Enter the gardens on your right.

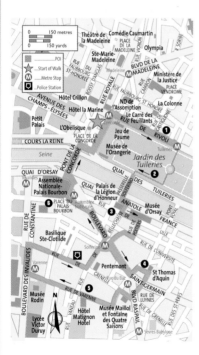

2 Jardin des Tuileries

Laid out in 1664 by Louis XIV's chief gardener, André Le Nôtre, the gardens soon became a popular place for strolling. The western end is quite elaborate, with its octagonal pool surrounded by statues, terraces and twin pavilions, while from the round pool at the other end the view extends all the way to the Champs-Élysées and the Arc de Triomphe.
The Terrasse du Bord de l'Eau, by the river, affords good views of the Left Bank. Cross Passerelle Solférino.

3 Palais de la Légion d'Honneur

Take rue de la Légion d'Honneur between the impressive Musée d'Orsay (to the left), which has a convenient restaurant, and the Musée National de la Légion d'Honneur (to the right), which illustrates the history of the orders of French Chivalry before the 1789

Revolution, and the Legion of Honour, which Napoleon founded in 1802.
Tel: 01 40 62 84 25. www.musee-legiondhonneur.fr. Open: Wed–Sun 1–6pm. Closed: Mon–Tue.
Turn left into rue de Lille and right into rue de Poitiers which leads to rue de l'Université. On reaching boulevard St-Germain, turn left, then turn left again into rue du Bac.

4 St-Thomas-d'Aquin

Begun in the 17th century and finished in the 18th, this church, on the left, was originally the chapel of a Dominican monastery. Inside are some fine 17th- and 18th-century paintings, which provide a perfect setting for the regular Sunday organ concerts.
Follow rue de Luynes to rue de Grenelle, and turn right past the elaborate Fontaine des Quatre Saisons (see p112). Turn left.

5 Rue de Varenne

The name of this street is derived from *gerenne* (warren), a reminder of the days when Faubourg St-Germain was a rural area. It is lined with several stately mansions: the most famous is the Hôtel Matignon at No 57, the prime minister's official residence since 1958. Built in 1721 and once owned by Talleyrand, it has the largest private gardens in Paris. Its contemporary, the Hôtel Biron at the end of the street, also has beautiful gardens. Today the Hôtel Biron houses a museum dedicated to the sculptor Rodin, who lived there.
Turn right, then right again into rue de Grenelle, taking a look at the smaller-scale Hôtel de Lillars at No 118. Turn left down rue de Bellechasse and left on boulevard St-Germain to bring you back to the river.

6 Palais Bourbon

The impressive Palais Bourbon is the seat of the Assemblée Nationale and was remodelled by Napoleon to match the Madeleine (*see p84*) facing it on the other side of place de la Concorde.
Cross Pont de la Concorde and place de la Concorde, then follow rue Royale towards the Madeleine.

Striking sculptural art provides an added attraction in the elegant Jardin des Tuileries

Zouave keeps a watchful eye on the water level at Pont de l'Alma

Parc Georges Brassens

Two bronze bulls at the main entrance are a reminder that this park was created on the site of the former Vaugirard slaughterhouses. A small garden filled with scented plants was specially designed for blind people, and the vineyard is the scene of festivities during the grape harvest in October.
Rue des Morillons, 75015.
Métro: Convention.

LUXEMBOURG AND PORT ROYAL
Fontaine de l'Observatoire

This bronze fountain by Davioud dates from 1873. It depicts the different parts of the world – Europe, Asia, Africa and America – but not Oceania, which would have spoilt the symmetry of the composition. It is also called Fontaine des Quatre Parties du Monde.
Avenue de l'Observatoire, 75006, south of the Luxembourg gardens.
RER: Port-Royal or Luxembourg.

Musée Zadkine

The works of the Russian-born sculptor Zadkine are exhibited in the house where he lived for 40 years until his death in 1967. The majority of his works reveal his anxious nature. The various studies he made of Van Gogh are of particular interest.
100 bis rue d'Assas. Tel: 01 55 42 77 20.
Open: Tue–Sun 10am–5.30pm. Closed: Mon. Admission charge. RER: Port-Royal.

Underground Paris
Catacombes (Catacombs)

The city's network of tunnels has many practical uses other than the métro, and part of it can be visited. In the 18th century Parisians found a new use for some underground galleries on the site of Roman stone quarries. They became a much-needed cemetery to relieve the overcrowded Cimetière des Innocents situated near Les Halles, where the Fontaine des Innocents now stands. The site was consecrated, and the bones were piled along the galleries. There are now guided visits to these catacombs.
Les Catacombes, 1 place Denfert-Rochereau, 75014. Tel: 01 43 22 47 63.
Open: Tue–Sun 10am–5pm. Closed: Mon. Admission charge.
Métro: Denfert-Rochereau.

Val-de-Grâce

Situated on the edge of the Quartier Latin, this 17th-century church was designed by Mansart in the Jesuit style fashionable at that time, with a two-tier façade, a dome modelled on St Peter's in Rome and, above all, superb Baroque decorations. Particularly remarkable are the huge baldachin resting on six twisted columns, and the painting in the cupola by Pierre Mignard. Following the Revolution the abbey became a military hospital.

Rue St-Jacques (boulevard de Port-Royal end), 75005. RER: Port-Royal or Luxembourg.

Parc Montsouris

Another of Haussmann's creations, this hilly park facing the Cité Universitaire (the student halls of residence) includes a large lake, waterfalls, a meteorological observatory and a reproduction of the Bardo, the Bey of Tunis' palace.
Boulevard Jourdan.
RER: Cité Universitaire.

Val-de-Grâce is one of Paris's best examples of Baroque architecture

Paris environs

The region around Paris is rich with beautiful palaces, châteaux and modern getaways that make for perfect day trips. From the lavish Versailles to historic Fontainebleau and the entertaining Disneyland® Paris, all visitors will find something that appeals to them. Further afield, too, lie a number of not-to-be-missed towns and attractions. Chartres is the 'acropolis' of medieval sculpture and architecture, while Chantilly and Vaux-le-Vicomte offer excellent cultural days out.

ÎLE-DE-FRANCE
Disneyland® Paris

At the heart of Disneyland® Resort Paris is the theme Disneyland® Park – only part of a vast holiday resort covering nearly 2,000ha (4,942 acres), one-fifth the size of Paris. Next to Disneyland® Park is the newly opened Walt Disney Studios® Park, a behind-the-scenes world of film, television and animation.

Disneyland® Park, with its five magical lands, is an amazing mixture of fantasy and adventure where you can meet Mickey Mouse, fly with Dumbo, explore the Swiss Family Robinson's tree house, be propelled to the moon through Space Mountain, and return to ground to follow the tracks of Indiana Jones™ and the Temple of Peril: Backwards. The most recent addition to the park's clutch of attractions is Toy Story Playland, which includes three new rides: Toy Soldiers Parachute Drop, Slinky Dog Zigzag Spin and RC Racer. Further new rides are scheduled for the big

anniversary in 2012. The resort also has seven themed hotels, a golf course and Disney® Village, which offers a whole range of restaurants and shops and plenty of entertainment for both day and night.
Marne-la-Vallée, 77700. Tel: 08 25 30 60 30. www.disneylandparis.com. Open: all year; daily timings vary with the seasons. Admission charge. RER (A): Chessy (end of the line).

Fontainebleau

Set at the heart of a splendid forest, this peaceful residential town lives in the shadow of its beautiful palace. A spring in the middle of the forest determined the choice of Fontainebleau as the site of a royal castle as far back as the 12th century.

The castle

François I transformed the austere medieval castle into a magnificent Renaissance residence, sparing no expense in decorating the new buildings

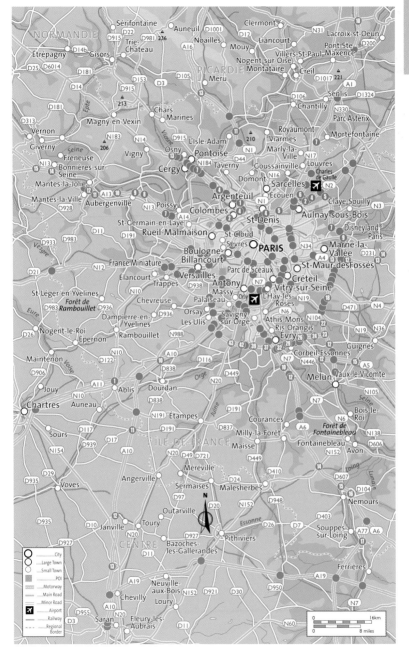

that form the central part of the palace, which was later extended by Henri IV.

Louis XIV, Louis XV and Louis XVI contributed further to the decoration of the apartments. Spared by the Revolution, the palace continued to be used by kings and emperors until the end of the 19th century, when it was turned into a museum.

The buildings surround four courtyards. Access to the palace is through the main courtyard, or **Cour du Cheval Blanc**. At the end of the courtyard is the famous 'horseshoe' staircase, from which Napoleon made a very emotional farewell to his imperial guard before his departure to Elba in 1814. Beyond is the **Cour de la Fontaine**, backed by the Galerie François I. The Cour de la Fontaine overlooks the Étang des Carpes, a small carp pond with a charming pavilion in its centre. Le Nôtre's formal garden is on one side of the pond, and the **Jardin Anglais** (English-style garden) is on the other side. In the centre of the latter is the Fontaine Bliaud. The oldest part of the palace surrounds the **Cour Ovale**. A monumental entrance gives access to the **Cour des Offices**, which is lined with outbuildings dating from 1609.

Inside, the **Grands Appartements** (state apartments) on the first floor start with the Galerie François I, with its original Renaissance decoration of stucco and frescoes. The Escalier du Roi leads to the magnificent Salle de Bal (ballroom); the ceiling and chimney piece are particularly remarkable.

On the other side of the Cour Ovale are the **Appartements Royaux**, the monarchs' private and official apartments, which include the Salon du Donjon, the only remaining part of the medieval castle, and the Salle du Trône, formerly the king's bedroom. In the emperor's official apartments is the famous Salon Rouge, where he abdicated in 1814.

The **Petits Appartements**, which are on the ground floor, were formerly the private apartments of Napoleon and Joséphine, and contain some splendid Empire furniture.

65km (40 miles) southeast of Paris. Entrance: place du Général de Gaulle. Tel: 01 60 71 50 70. www.musee-

Double horseshoe staircase, Fontainebleau

WILDLIFE

You do not have to be a connoisseur to appreciate the subtle blend of colours and the fresh scent of woodland flowers in springtime. In the verdant Forêt de Fontainebleau, hyacinths, daffodils and laburnum herald the return of warm weather, followed by hawthorn blossoms and fragile lilies-of-the-valley. Later on, dense bushes of gorse light up the green undergrowth, eclipsing the more discreet heather, campanulas and wild carnations. Summer offers the pleasure of looking for wild strawberries and raspberries, while autumn brings hazelnuts and chestnuts. These traditional hunting grounds still abound with roe deer and boar, as well as the more common foxes, hares and squirrels. There is also a great variety of birdlife, including the famous Fontainebleau woodpeckers.

château-fontainebleau.fr. Open: Wed–Mon 9.30am–5pm (winter); Wed–Mon 9.30am–6pm (summer). Closed: Tue. Admission charge.

Forêt de Fontainebleau

This vast forest surrounding the castle and town of Fontainebleau over an area of 25,000ha (61,774 acres) offers a landscape of wooded hills and valleys, of moors covered with heather and gorse, and of large rocks piled high in places. Pines, oaks and beeches make up the majority of the forest. There are opportunities for rock climbing and the area has become popular with amateurs and professionals.

Various itineraries are suggested in the *Guide des sentiers de promenades dans le massif forestier de Fontainebleau*, available from the tourist office in Fontainebleau. Most tours start from the town. To the west are the Gorges de Franchard, a narrow glen scattered with impressive overhanging rocks. To the south, Le Long Rocher is a rock-strewn plateau that affords lovely views over the forest. *60km (37 miles) southeast of Paris.*

Forêt de Rambouillet

Although less spectacular than Fontainebleau, this forest, covering 20,000ha (49,419 acres), offers pleasant walks and cycle tours through ancient villages, along narrow rivers and beside picturesque lakes. Oak and pine predominate, and red deer and wild boar are plentiful, if not always easy to detect.

In the isolated northern part of the forest, fishermen seek peace and quiet on the shores of the Étang Neuf, near the solitary 16th-century castle of La Mormaire and the almost deserted village of Gambaiseuil. Further south, from the Rochers d'Angennes, a rock formation on high ground, there is a

Spend the day in Fontainebleau forest

Walk or cycle in the Forêt de Rambouillet

good view of the Étang d'Angennes, overgrown with reeds, and the secluded valley of the Guesle River.
44km (27 miles) southwest of Paris.

France Miniature

This theme park will take you on a lightning journey across France, travelling from one region to the next in a few minutes. Two thousand models reduced 30 times, including 168 monuments, 20 typical villages, landscapes and scenes of daily life, are spread over a vast relief map of France that covers 5ha (12 acres).

There are shops selling crafts and other products from the regions of France, exhibitions, stands where you can sample regional cuisine, a picnic area and two restaurants.

25 route du Mesnil, Élancourt. Tel: 01 30 16 16 30. www.franceminiature.fr. Open: Apr–Jun & Sept–Oct 10am–6pm, Jul–Aug 10am–7pm. Closed: Nov–Mar and certain days at other times, so check first. Admission charge. RER: St-Quentin-en-Yvelines, then shuttle service to the theme park.

L'Haÿ-les-Roses

Situated in the densely populated southern suburbs, halfway between Paris and Orly Airport, the rose garden of L'Haÿ-les-Roses was created 100 years ago; thousands of roses, wild as well as hybrids, offer a grand display of colours in a charming setting framed with climbers. There is also a Musée de la Rose devoted to works of art connected with this aristocratic flower:

prints, embroidery, ceramics and small objets d'art.
8km (5 miles) south of Paris.
Admission charge.

Malmaison

Situated 10km (6 miles) west of Paris, the elegant 17th-century Château de Malmaison is famous for its connection with Napoleon. His first wife, Joséphine de Beauharnais, bought the castle in 1799, and Napoleon always loved the place. When he divorced her in 1809 to marry Marie-Louise of Austria, Joséphine kept Malmaison for a short while until her death in 1814. Napoleon revisited the castle when he escaped from the island of Elba and returned to France, and again just before he was finally exiled on the island of St Helena.

The castle had many owners before it was eventually donated to the nation and turned into a museum, housing mementoes of Napoleon and Joséphine. Some of the original furniture from their various residences is on display. Behind the castle is a lovely park and forest, perfect for a stroll or picnic after your visit.
Musée National du Château de Malmaison, avenue du Château, 92500 Rueil-Malmaison. Tel: 01 41 29 05 55. Open: Mon & Wed–Fri 10am–5.45pm, Sat–Sun 10am–6.15pm (summer); Mon & Wed–Fri 10am–12.30pm & 1.30–5.15pm, Sat–Sun 10am–12.30pm & 1.30–5.45pm (winter). Closed: Tue. Admission charge. RER: La Défense. Bus: 258 to Le Château.

The nearby **Château de Bois-Préau**, which also belonged to Joséphine, is devoted to mementoes of Napoleon's exile on the island of St Helena.
1 avenue de l'Impératrice Joséphine, 92500 Rueil-Malmaison. Tel: 01 41 29 05 55. www.château-malmaison.fr. Open: Wed–Mon 10am–12.30pm & 1.30–5.15pm. Closed: Tue.

Parc de St-Cloud

Situated in one of the elegant western suburbs overlooking the Seine, this park was designed by Le Nôtre. The castle, where Napoleon stayed many times, was destroyed by fire in 1870. The Grande Cascade, with its statues featuring the Seine and the Marne rivers, is particularly remarkable; so is the view across Paris from the terrace. The woods in the upper part of the park offer lovely cool walks in summer.
On the N186, 11km (6¾ miles) west of Paris.

Parc de Sceaux

The gardens were designed by Le Nôtre, and Louis XIV was invited to a splendid reception to mark the inauguration of the castle, built in 1670. During the Revolution the estate was bought for the use of the land and the castle was demolished. The state acquired the property in 1923, and undertook its restoration.

Once more water is the focal point of the beautiful gardens: on the south side a wide avenue leads to the Grandes Cascades, a succession of waterfalls supplying an octagonal lake surrounded by plane trees reflected in the still water; the grand canal is also lined with trees, which create contrasts of sunlight and shade, and temper the formal aspect of French-style gardens.

The Petit Château and the Pavillon de l'Aurore (in the northeast corner of the park) date from the 17th century. In the latter there is an audiovisual presentation of the estate.

10km (6 miles) southwest of Paris.

St-Denis

This industrialised and somewhat rough northern suburb is worth the visit for its beautiful Gothic cathedral, where most French monarchs have been buried.

The first bishop of Paris, Saint Denis, martyred in Montmartre, is said to have walked, holding his head in his hands, to a field where he died and was buried. His grave soon became a place of pilgrimage, and the first church was built there in the 5th century; then, in 630, King Dagobert founded a powerful abbey to control the growing numbers of pilgrims. He was buried in the new church, which became the traditional burial place of his successors.

Abbot Suger is closely linked to the history of the present cathedral. Born of poor parents, he was taken into care by the abbey. His exceptional gifts having won him the confidence of Louis VII, he became abbot of St-Denis in 1122 and designed a great Gothic

cathedral that served as a prototype for later masterpieces such as Chartres Cathedral. The edifice was completed in just over ten years. During the second half of the 13th century Saint Louis had the nave and transept rebuilt by Pierre de Montreuil, the architect of the Sainte-Chapelle, but the beautiful façade remained unaltered.

Grossly neglected over the centuries, the cathedral suffered great damage during the 1789 Revolution. Restoration work carried out in the 19th century involved the pulling down of the north tower. Viollet-le-Duc, who also restored Notre-Dame, finally undertook to save what was left.

The façade looks mutilated without its north tower. The base of the towers, over the rose window, is crenellated – a reminder that the edifice was originally fortified. The tympanum of the main portal illustrates the *Last Judgement*, the other two being connected with Saint Denis.

The cathedral is, above all, a museum of the French monarchy, with its numerous funeral monuments carved by the greatest sculptors. In the 13th century Saint Louis commissioned monuments for his predecessors, the most remarkable being Dagobert's imposing tomb. It became the tradition for later kings to have their own grave designed. Some, dating from the Renaissance, are particularly elaborate, such as the monument commissioned by Catherine de' Medici for herself and Henri II.

In the Romanesque crypt is the collective grave of all the Bourbons. *Place de l'Hôtel de Ville, 93200 St-Denis. Tel: 01 48 09 83 54. Open: Apr–Sept Mon–Sat 10am–6.15pm, Sun noon–6.15pm; Oct–Mar Mon–Sat 10am–5pm, Sun noon–5.15pm. Métro: St-Denis-Basilique.*

St-Germain-en-Laye

This important residential town, 18km (11 miles) west of Paris, has a history going back to the building of the first castle in the 12th century. The Renaissance castle, erected in 1539 by Pierre Chambiges on the same site, was later extended by Jules Hardouin-Mansart, and the park and gardens were designed by Le Nôtre, including a magnificent Grande Terrasse, 2.4km (1½ miles) long.

In 1855, Napoleon III restored the castle to its original state and set up the **Musée des Antiquités Nationales**. The museum's archaeological collections cover France's past from the Palaeolithic period to the Dark Ages, and include a reconstruction of the famous Salle des Taureaux at Lascaux. *Place du Château. Tel: 01 39 10 13 00. Museum open: Wed–Mon 9am–5.15pm. Closed: Tue. Admission charge. RER: St-Germain-en-Laye.*

Sèvres

This small town, 10km (6 miles) west of Paris, has become synonymous with beautiful china. The Manufacture Nationale de Porcelaine began making fine porcelain here in the 18th century. Its specialities include the famous *bleu*

The castle museum of St-Germain-en-Laye

de Sèvres, a deep blue on a pure white background, and exquisite *biscuits*, unglazed delicate statuettes.

Founded in 1824, the **Musée National de la Céramique** contains precious exhibits from all over the world.
Place de la Manufacture, 92310 Sèvres.
Tel: 01 49 29 22 00.
www.sevresciteceramique.fr.
Open: Wed–Mon 10am–5pm.
Closed: Tue. Admission charge.
Métro: Pont de Sèvres.

Vallée de Chevreuse

The upper valley of the River Yvette is known as the Vallée de Chevreuse after the small town dominated by the ruins of its castle. In 1984 a regional park was created to preserve this area of natural beauty, consisting of woodland, lush meadows and cultivated land. The D58, which follows the river westwards, leads to the Château de Dampierre (*see p137*). To the north are the ruins of the Cistercian abbey of Port-Royal-des-Champs, famous in the 17th century for its criticism of the Jesuits. The southern road (D24) leads to Les Vaux de Cernay, where a picturesque stream makes its way through woods and rocks.
The town of Chevreuse is situated 30km (19 miles) southwest of Paris.

Versailles

For most people, the palace of Versailles is the supreme example of an aspect of French culture that blends elegance and refinement with a search for perfection – sometimes coupled with excessive formality and strikingly bold confidence.

In 1661 Louis XIV, the 'Sun King', decided to build a castle that would outshine Vaux-le-Vicomte (*see p141*) on the site of the modest brick-and-stone château built by Philibert Le Roy for his father in 1631.

For nearly 50 years the greatest artists worked at Versailles: the architect Le Vau, succeeded by Hardouin-Mansart; Le Brun, who supervised the interior decoration; and Le Nôtre, who surpassed himself in the design of the magnificent gardens. The king and his court moved in during 1682 – a total of 3,000 people, attending sumptuous receptions. From 1682 to 1789 Versailles was also the political centre of France.

During the Revolution the furniture was sold, and the château gradually fell into disrepair until, in 1837, Louis-Philippe had it converted into a museum of French history.

After World War I total restoration of the castle was undertaken with the financial help of US philanthropist J D Rockefeller, and Versailles has slowly regained its 18th-century elegance.

The castle

The approach to the château, one of the most visited monuments in France, is very impressive. There is a succession of three open courtyards to be traversed, the Court of Ministers, the Royal Court and the Court of Marble, with Louis XIV's statue in the centre.

On the garden side, the 680m (2,231ft)-long façade has a projecting central section. An elegant balustrade emphasises the roof line, and groups of graceful columns at regular intervals attract the eye as focal points.

State Apartments

On the way to the State Apartments, take a look at the chapel. This was designed by Hardouin-Mansart but only completed after his death in 1710.

The State Apartments include a suite of reception rooms, decorated with marble and paintings; they were used for the entertainment of the court during the winter season.

The large windows of the 75m (246ft)-long Galerie des Glaces (Hall of Mirrors) overlook the gardens and let in the setting sun. The sunlight reflects across the huge mirrors that cover the room's walls.

Next come the Queen's Apartments, in particular the Queen's bedroom where Louis XV and many royal children were born. The bedroom, remodelled by Louis XIV, was used by his successors until 1789. Next door is the Chambre du Conseil (Council Chamber).

Château de Versailles, place d'Armes. Tel: 01 30 83 78 00. www.chateauversailles.fr. Château open: daily 9am–5.30pm (winter); 9am–6.30pm (summer). Park open: 8am–dusk (winter); 7am–dusk (summer). RER: Versailles-Rive gauche. Admission charge, which includes a complimentary audio guide.

One of the exquisite ceilings in the château at Versailles

Visits – without guide: Chapel & State Apartments, from entrance A on the right; with guide: Appartement du Roi, last visit starts at 4pm. Appartements du Dauphin et de la Dauphine et de Mesdames: guided visits during daylight hours. Events: Every Sat–Sun Apr–Sept, there is a spectacular fountain show, with music, 11am–noon & 3.30–5pm. Combined fountains and firework displays are also held on some Saturday nights in summer.

Cabinets Intérieurs du Roi

The king's private apartments, designed by the Parisian architect Ange-Jacques Gabriel for Louis XV, include the bedroom where the king died in 1774, the study with its original desk, the music room in which the young Wolfgang Mozart is supposed to have played in 1763, and the beautiful library.

Open: daily 9am–5pm (winter); 9am–6pm (summer).

The **Cabinets Intérieurs de la Reine** were private apartments originally designed for Louis XV's queen, and were later refurbished for Marie-Antoinette. *Cabinets Intérieurs de la Reine: guided tours: daily 9am–5pm (winter); 9am–6pm (summer).*

Opéra Royal

Also built by Gabriel, the opera house was inaugurated in 1770 for the wedding of Marie-Antoinette to the future Louis XVI. It could seat 700 spectators and could also be used as a grand reception room or a ballroom. On the ground floor are the recently renovated Appartements du Dauphin et de la Dauphine (the heirs to the throne), and those of Louis XV's daughters.

Waterways and fountains in the gardens at Versailles

Opéra Royal: hour-long guided visits – last one starting at 4pm.

The gardens
From the raised terrace in front of the château, the Grand Canal offers a magnificent vista that extends to the woods in the distance. The design of the gardens by Le Nôtre, between 1661 and 1668, is a masterpiece of geometry: the canal is the focal point of a composition on different levels, of ornamental ponds adorned with fountains, flowerbeds, bowers and over 200 sculptures.

The Trianons
The Trianons are lesser palaces located in the wooded part of the gardens. The Grand Trianon, faced with pink marble, was built by Hardouin-Mansart for Louis XIV, who wished to give private receptions for Madame de Maintenon.

The Petit Trianon was commissioned by Louis XV and given by Louis XVI to Marie-Antoinette, who used it to be alone with her children. She had the garden completely remodelled and the charming *hameau* (hamlet) built nearby. *Grand and Petit Trianons: open: daily 9am–5.30pm (winter); 9am–6.30pm (summer). Entrance A on the right.*

FURTHER AFIELD
Chantilly
Situated north of Paris on the edge of an ancient forest, in the heart of horse-racing country, the Château de Chantilly is surrounded by a beautiful park with ponds and lakes.

Château de Chantilly
The castle The history of the castle goes back to Roman times: Cantilius was the first nobleman to build a fortified house on the site. In the 16th century the house was replaced by a castle with a splendid Renaissance edifice, and the Petit Château was built next to it. In 1662 Le Nôtre remodelled the gardens and park. One of Louis Philippe's sons, the Duc d'Aumale, rebuilt the Grand Château, which had been damaged during the Revolution. On his death in 1897 he left the whole estate to the nation, including his magnificent art collections, which form the basis of the Condé museum.

The museum In the Petit Château are the former private apartments. The library contains *Les Très Riches Heures du Duc de Berry*, a precious 15th-century illuminated Book of Hours. In the chapel there is an altar carved by Jean Goujon, and some 16th-century stained glass.

In the Grand Château there are paintings by Poussin, Corot, Raphael, Watteau, Ingres and Botticelli, a unique collection of portraits by Clouet, father and son, and the famous Grand Condé diamond, which was stolen in 1926 but found later in an apple where it had been hidden by the thieves.

The park Most of Le Nôtre's masterpiece of landscape gardening remains: the grand canal and its waterfall, and the shorter canal lined with formal gardens leading to the raised terrace. The *hameau* (hamlet), added in the 18th century, is similar to the more famous one in Versailles. The Jardin Anglais (English garden) was designed in 1820.

The Grandes Ecuries The vast stable was designed in the 18th century to house 250 horses, 500 dogs and 100 attendants. It is now a museum. The *Prix du Jockey-Club-Lancia* and the *Prix de Diane-Hermès* are run every June on the stable's beautiful racecourse.
35km (22 miles) north of Paris.
Tel: 03 44 27 31 80.
www.museevivantducheval.fr. Open:
Wed–Mon 2–5pm (Dec–Mar); Wed–
Mon 10am–5pm (Apr–Nov).
Closed: Tue. Admission charge.

Chartres

Chartres is the main town of the vast plain of La Beauce, 85km (53 miles) southwest of Paris. In the centre of the old town, on the left bank of the River Eure, stands one of the most beautiful cathedrals in France. Rebuilt in the space of 25 years after a fire destroyed part of the Romanesque edifice in 1194, and spared by wars and revolutions, the cathedral is a unique example of French early Gothic style showing remarkable architectural unity. Pilgrims have been flocking to Chartres since medieval times and, in 1935, students started their own pilgrimage, which takes place every year at the end of April.

Chartres Cathedral
The originality of the façade stems from the contrast between the sombre outline of the Clocher Vieux on the right, in pure Romanesque style, and the rich decoration of the slightly taller spire of the Clocher Neuf, added in 1506. The Portail Royal, famous for its series of tall, column-like figures, and the three windows above it are 12th century, the rest being 13th century. The portals of the north and south transepts, dating from the 13th century, are equally remarkable.

The proportions of the interior are vast, with an overall length of 130m (427ft) and a height of 37m (121ft). The Gothic nave, the widest in France, appears relatively short in comparison

Chartres Cathedral, a magnet for pilgrims

with the transept and chancel. In the faint light, the deep, rich colours of the stained-glass windows, dating from the 12th and 13th centuries, immediately capture the attention. The elaborate choir-screen, with its 41 groups of sculptures depicting the life of Christ and the Virgin Mary, was designed in 1514 by Jehan de Beauce. The crypt is the largest in France and the oldest part of the cathedral. There are traces of a Gallo-Roman wall and a deep well.

The old town between the cathedral and the river has been renovated, and offers a pleasant journey back in time, especially along rue des Écuyers and its adjacent streets.

Open: 9am–6pm. Admission charge to the crypt and gallery of the Clocher Neuf.

Courances

The Château de Courances lies 55km (34 miles) south of Paris in wooded country. It is near the small town of Milly-la-Forêt, famous for its beautiful 15th-century covered market.

The original Renaissance castle was remodelled in the early 17th century into a fine example of Louis XIII style. The intricate design of the brick panels, accentuated by stone borders, is offset by the absence of decoration, while the steep slate roofs add an interesting contrast of colour. The outline of the strictly symmetrical edifice is enhanced by the softness of the green setting, reflected in the water of the moat and artificial lakes. A copy of the famous staircase at Fontainebleau was added in the 19th century. The castle is still inhabited and only open at weekends.

The gardens were planned by Le Nôtre, who gave a romantic aspect to his masterly design through the use of reflection in the water of several canals supplied by the nearby École River. *Guided visits on Sat–Sun 2.30–6pm, from Apr–Oct. Tel: 01 64 98 41 18. Admission charge. This visit can be combined with that of the Château de Fontainebleau, 17km (11 miles) to the east.*

Dampierre

About 36km (22 miles) southwest of Paris, Dampierre-en-Yvelines is a small community situated at the heart of the Parc Naturel Régional de la Haute Vallée de Chevreuse, a protected rural area. The castle stands out against the dark wooded setting of the vast park laid out by Le Nôtre.

The 16th-century castle, rebuilt in the late 17th century for Colbert's son-in-law, has been the property of the Luynes family ever since; it was restored during the first half of the 19th century. The elegant brick-and-stone façade is flanked by two arcaded buildings on either side.

The ground-floor reception rooms have Louis XIV and Louis XV wood panelling. On the first floor are the royal apartments, splendidly decorated to honour the monarchs who stayed at Dampierre on various occasions: Louis XIV, Louis XV and Louis XVI. At the top of the monumental staircase, the large reception room, decorated with murals by Ingres, is most remarkable. A colourful floral garden occupies part of the park.

Château de Dampierre. Tel: 01 30 52 53 24. www.château-de-dampierre.fr. Open: Apr–Sept daily 11am–6.30pm. Admission charge.

Écouen

Écouen is a peaceful community in the green belt surrounding Paris. Barely 20km (12 miles) north of the city, it is famous for its Renaissance castle, which houses the **Musée National de la Renaissance (Renaissance Museum)**.

The castle was built in the early 16th century for Anne de Montmorency. Like Chantilly, it became the property of the Condé family from whom it was confiscated during the French Revolution. It was later used by Napoleon as a school for the daughters of members of the Légion d'Honneur. The façade is adorned with columns and surmounted by dormer windows with carved pediments. It has recently been turned into a museum of Renaissance art to relieve the overcrowded Musée National du Moyen Âge (*see pp52–3*).

The building itself is a wonderful representation of the Renaissance era. Furniture, wood panels, tapestries, ceramics – 8,000 exhibits in all are displayed in 34 rooms, which have retained their original decoration whenever possible, in particular their painted mantelpieces. On the ground

Handsomely proportioned Dampierre Castle

floor there is a superb collection of arms; on the first floor, the private apartments of Montmorency and his wife have some interesting furniture, while a fine 75m (246ft)-long 16th-century tapestry, takes up the whole of one wing. On the second floor there are numerous 16th- and 17th-century ceramic compositions, stained-glass painted wood panels and enamels.

Château d'Écouen. Tel: 01 34 38 38 50. www.musee-renaissance.fr. Open: Wed–Mon 9.30am–12.45pm & 2–5.15pm (winter); Wed–Mon 9.30am–12.45pm & 2–5.45pm (summer). Closed: Tue. Admission charge. This visit can be combined with an excursion to the Château de Chantilly.

Giverny

This village, situated near the town of Vernon, 80km (50 miles) west of Paris, has strong links with Impressionism through one of the main exponents of the movement, the painter Claude Monet, who lived there from 1883 until his death in 1926. His house has been turned into a museum containing mementoes of the artist and the friends and colleagues who were his guests. While no original paintings of the artist are on display, visitors can admire his impressive collection of Japanese prints. The garden, which he designed himself, inspired many of his paintings, including the huge *Nymphéas* exhibited in the Musée de l'Orangerie (*see p40*).

Claude Monet's famous garden at Giverny

Maison de Claude Monet. Tel: 02 32 51 28 21. www.fondation-monet.com. Open: Apr–Oct daily 9.30am–6pm. Admission charge.

Royaumont

The Cistercian abbey of Royaumont, founded by Saint Louis in 1228 and richly endowed by his successors, remained powerful until the Revolution. The church was then demolished, and the extensive abbey buildings turned into a cotton mill. Royaumont, now owned by a foundation, is the scene of regular cultural activities.

Very little remains of the church. Next to it the cloister, which encloses a garden, is the largest of any Cistercian abbey in France. The long refectory, where Saint Louis served the monks himself during his visits to the abbey, is a masterpiece of early Gothic architecture. In the kitchens, the impressive vaulted ceiling rests on massive columns boasting fine carved capitals.

30km (19 miles) north of Paris. Tel: 01 30 35 59 70. www.royaumont.com. Open: daily 10am–6pm. Admission charge. This excursion can be combined with a trip to Chantilly.

The Épidemaïs Croisière boat ride runs through Parc Astérix

Parc Astérix

The setting is France under Roman occupation 2,000 years ago, seen through the eyes of the characters created by Albert Uderzo for his series of *Astérix* comic strips, in which the intelligent and cunning Gauls constantly outwit the dumb Romans.

Asterix, the hero, is the brain behind the action, and Obelix, his fat, devoted friend, lends him his muscle power, with Getafix the druid and many others. But there is more. Parc Astérix is an adventure park with many outdoor activities for the whole family; there are shops in Via Antiqua and rue de Paris, a medieval square with its crowd of jugglers and acrobats, and two restaurants.

60128 Plailly. Tel: 08 92 68 30 10. www.parcasterix.fr.
Opening times vary: see website for details. Closed: Feb–Mar. Admission charge. RER: Roissy–Charles de Gaulle I, then shuttle service to the park.

Vaux-le-Vicomte

Situated 51km (32 miles) southeast of Paris, the castle of Vaux-le-Vicomte is a masterpiece of 17th-century French architecture. Fouquet, Louis XIV's finance minister, had gathered a colossal fortune and decided to build a castle that would be a symbol of his success. In 1656 he commissioned the best artists of his time, and an army of 18,000 workers completed the castle in just five years. Fouquet invited Louis XIV to a splendid reception that greatly surpassed those given at court. Dishes of solid gold crowned dozens of buffet tables set out in the garden, while jewel-studded elephants lined the alleys of orange trees, and Chinese fireworks were shot off from the ponds. The king was so annoyed that he had Fouquet – who had already fallen from favour – arrested a few days later. After a lengthy trial the ambitious minister was condemned to life imprisonment. The castle changed hands several times during the next 200 years until it was bought by a rich industrialist, whose family have since restored both house and gardens.

The main building stands on a raised terrace surrounded by a moat. On the ground floor, six reception rooms on either side of the oval Grand Salon (drawing room) overlook the magnificent gardens. The frescoes on the ceilings, depicting mythological scenes, are by Le Brun. A staircase in the entrance hall gives access to the first-floor private apartments. From the terrace the view sweeps across the gardens, which are adorned with ornamental ponds, cascades and a Grand Canal. In the stables there is a museum of horse-drawn carriages.

Vaux-le-Vicomte, 77950 Maincy, near Melun. Tel: 01 64 14 41 90. www.vaux-le-vicomte.com.
Open: end Mar to mid-Nov daily 10am–6pm. Admission charge. Saturday candlelit visits from May–Sept 8pm–midnight. Cafeteria. RER: Melun, then by shuttle service or taxi for 6km (3¾ miles).

Shopping

Part of the fun of staying in Paris is the opportunity to go on a shopping spree. Deciding where to go, however, can be quite bewildering in any large city, and particularly in Paris where attractive shop windows are to be found round every street corner. While sales are strictly regulated and only take place twice a year (generally in January and in July), there are plenty of opportunities for a bargain. Big department stores will often have special offers linked to a particular event or an individual product.

Before you embark on a shopping tour of Paris there are a few facts you should be aware of.

It is dangerous to carry large amounts of cash, as pickpockets frequent crowded places. The safest and most widely used method of payment in boutiques, department stores and shopping centres is by credit card; but bear in mind that a minimum purchase is often required. Be prepared to pay cash at market stalls and food kiosks.

Although shops remain open quite late in the evening (*see p184*), individual shops are often closed on Monday morning, or sometimes all day Monday. So, if planning a long weekend in Paris, it is better to opt for Friday rather than Monday.

Department stores

Most of Paris's large department stores are situated on the right bank. Moreover, Parisians often refer to the St-Lazare-Opéra district as the *quartier des grands magasins*, as the most prestigious of them are lined up along boulevard Haussmann.

Galeries Lafayette (*40 boulevard Haussmann, 75009, tel: 01 42 82 34 56, métro: Chaussée d'Antin*) and **Le Printemps** (*64 boulevard Haussmann, tel: 01 42 82 50 00, www.printemps.com, métro: Havre-Caumartin*) tend to lay emphasis more and more on elegance and fashion trends in clothes and accessories, as well as household goods.

The Louvre and the Hôtel de Ville, along the rue de Rivoli, also house a couple of department stores. The **Bazar de l'Hôtel de Ville**, known as the BHV (*52 rue de Rivoli, 75004, tel: 01 42 74 90 00, www.bhv.fr, métro: Hôtel de Ville*), has a very well-stocked DIY department, as well as clothing, perfume, furniture and stationery.

Le Bon Marché (*22 rue de Sèvres, 75007, tel: 01 44 39 80 00, www. lebonmarche.com, métro: Sèvres-Babylone*) is the only department store on the left bank. It is rightly famous for its fine food section, **L'Épicerie**, which is open longer hours than the main store itself.

Arcades

Quaint and full of atmosphere, the arcades offer a change from traditional shopping (*see p77*).

Open-air markets

Not only do open-air markets offer good quality and low prices when it comes to fresh food, but they are also often the very fibre of a district's social life – a meeting place where neighbours of different backgrounds can exchange opinions.

These markets usually take place two or three mornings a week on a square or large open space. Two can be found in the Latin Quarter – on place Monge (*métro: Monge*) and place Maubert (*métro: Maubert-Mutualité*).

Covered markets

Steeped in tradition, these are the direct descendants of medieval structures known as *halles*, which usually consisted of a solid roof resting on large wooden pillars. Today there are 13 covered markets in Paris, all to be found on the right bank except one, which is situated in rue Mabillon in St-Germain-des-Prés (*métro: Mabillon*).

Specialised markets

The loveliest flower market in Paris is situated on place Louis Lépine, on the northern side of Île de la Cité (*métro:*

Cité) every day from 8am to 7pm, except on Sunday when it is replaced by a bird market. There is also a small pet market along quai de la Mégisserie on the right bank (*métro: Châtelet or Pont Neuf*).

On the corner of avenue de Marigny and avenue Gabriel (*métro: Champs-Élysées-Clemenceau*), an extensive stamp market takes place on Thursday, Saturday and Sunday.

Cheap new and second-hand clothes are sold in a covered market every morning except Monday on Carreau du Temple (*métro: Temple*).

Galeries Lafayette: shop till you drop

Flea markets

The most famous flea market in Paris is the Marché aux Puces of Porte de Clignancourt, in St-Ouen, which takes place on Saturday, Sunday and Monday between 7.30am and 7pm, though bargains are very rare these days. Other, similar but more genuine, markets are held in the open on Saturday and Sunday along avenues Georges Lafenestre and Marc Sangnier (*métro: Porte de Vanves*), and avenue de la Porte de Montreuil (*métro: Porte de Montreuil*).

For a current schedule and information about the *brocante* (vintage antiques) fairs that take place every weekend across different parts of town, *see www.paris.fr*

Shopping centres

The **Forum des Halles**, rue Pierre Lescot (*métro: Les Halles, see pp25–6*), is an underground complex with shops of all sizes selling just about everything from *foie gras* to shoes. The **Galeries des Champs-Élysées**, on the north side of the famous avenue (*métro: Franklin-Roosevelt*), are worth exploring for their elegant boutiques, as is the vast shopping complex at La Défense, **Les Quatre Temps**, which has a network of lanes lined with shops on several levels and a huge **Auchan** hypermarket.

Shopping streets and markets

Each district has an open-air market as well as one or two streets where food shops are concentrated. Customers are invited to select what they want. At these, prices can vary considerably.

The following streets are renowned for good quality and good value:
Near Les Halles: rue Montorgueil, which still keeps alive the atmosphere of the old Halles central food market (*see pp25–6*), and rue Rambuteau.
In the 17th *arrondissement*: rue Poncelet near place des Ternes, where there is one of the best coffee shops in Paris, the Brûlerie des Ternes at No 10.
In the 16th *arrondissement*: rue de l'Annonciation.
On the left bank: rue Mouffetard, rue de Buci and rue de Seine.

Specialised shops

Cheese can be bought in supermarkets, *épiceries* (grocers) and from market stalls. However, connoisseurs prefer to select from one of the more than 500 different cheeses made in France by buying from a reputed *fromager* who can recommend the best. **Androuët** (*41 rue d'Amsterdam, 75008; métro: Liège*) is something of a legend, with over 200 varieties in store.

Lionel Poilâne (*8 rue du Cherche-Midi, 75006; métro: Sèvres-Babylone*) is undoubtedly Paris's most famous bakery, while the *pâtisserie* **Lenôtre** (*48 avenue Victor Hugo, 75016; métro: Victor-Hugo, plus several other locations*) is unequalled for imagination and refinement. **Ladurée** (*21 rue Bonaparte, 75006 and other locations; tel: 01 44 07 64 87; www.laduree.fr*) is definitely an institution in Paris. Its pastel-coloured windows and ostensibly infinite variety of treats seem to beg a visit. **Berthillon** (*31 rue St-Louis-en-l'Île, 75004; métro: Pont Marie*) is the best place for ice cream, offering as it does many unusual flavours.

The Madeleine area (*métro: Madeleine*) has several luxury food shops, including the famous **Fauchon** (*26 place de la Madeleine*), an *épicerie fine* (luxury grocer) and delicatessen whose displays are real works of art, and the more modest **Hédiard** at No 21. Next door at No 19 is the **Maison de la Truffe**, where you can buy fresh truffles as well as delicious *charcuterie*. Further on is **Maille** at No 6 for fresh mustard and other condiments. Nearby, in rue Vignon, is the **Maison du Miel** at No 24, where you can taste and buy all kinds of rare honey.

Specialised streets and areas

In the 9th *arrondissement* there are busy shopping streets north of boulevard Haussmann, with a number of stamp collectors, high-class confectioners, upmarket decorators and fashion boutiques. Not far from there, in the 8th *arrondissement*, the area around place de l'Europe is well known for its musical-instrument makers and dealers.

South of boulevard Haussmann, avenue Matignon and rue du Faubourg St-Honoré are famous for their art galleries, while avenue Montaigne and rue François I are the headquarters of

fashion designers; rue de la Paix and place Vendôme are lined with exclusive jewellers. The main glass and china manufacturers have their showrooms along rue de Paradis, near Gare de l'Est in the 10th *arrondissement*.

Trade exhibitions

The **Chambre de Commerce et d'Industrie de Paris** (*tel: 08 20 01 20 12*) and **Foires, Salons et Congrès de France** (*tel: 01 53 90 20 00, www.fscef.com*) publish a list of trade exhibitions in Paris, which includes:

Foire à la Ferraille de Paris: literally a 'scrap-iron fair', in fact an antiques fair held in February, May and September in the Parc Floral de Paris.
Bois de Vincennes, 75012.
Métro: Château de Vincennes.

Foire Internationale de Paris: includes tourism, books, gardens, wines, sports and entertainment; held in May at the Parc des Expositions de Paris.
Porte de Versailles, 75015.
Métro: Porte de Versailles.

Musicora: this international exhibition of classical music is held during April in the Grand Palais.
Avenue Winston Churchill, 75008.
Métro: Champs-Élysées-Clémenceau.

Salon du Cheval et du Poney: all about horses, with various activities and show-jumping, held in December at the Parc des Expositions de Paris.

Salon Nautique International: popular boat show, held just before Christmas at the Parc des Expositions de Paris.

Antiques – worth a glance, browse or buy

WHERE TO SHOP
Antiques
Drouot

Famous auctioneers. Salerooms at:
9 rue Drouot. Tel: 01 48 00 20 20.
Métro: Richelieu-Drouot & Le Petetier.
15 avenue Montaigne. Tel: 01 48 00 20
80. Métro: Alma-Marceau.

Le Louvre des Antiquaires

250 shops offer plenty of choice, from
French furniture to jewellery.
2 place du Palais Royal, opposite
the Louvre. Tel: 01 42 97 27 27.
www.louvre-antiquaires.com.
Métro: Palais-Royal.

Village St Paul

More than 50 antique dealers are
established in the tiny pedestrian streets.
You can buy old prints and postcards
from the booksellers on the quais along
the Seine.
Métro: St-Paul or Pont Marie.

The Village Suisse

More than 100 dealers sell good-quality
ornaments and furniture.
78 avenue de Suffren. Tel: 01 43 06 69
90. www.levillagesuisseparis.com.
Métro: La Motte-Picquet-Grenelle.

Books

The largest bookshops in Paris are the
book departments of the **FNAC** stores
in *boulevard St-Germain, Forum des*
Halles and *avenue des Ternes.*

The 6th *arrondissement*, in and
around the boulevard St-Germain,
has many traditional bookshops.
Must-stop bookshops for literary
travellers include:

Shakespeare & Co

This famous bookshop is actually the
second in Paris under that name.
37 Rue Bucherie. Tel: 01 43 25 40 93.
www.shakespeareandco.com.
Métro: Cluny-La Sorbonne.

The Red Wheelbarrow

A charming, small but well-stocked
bookshop just across the road from
the Village St Paul.
22 Rue St Paul. Tel: 01 48 04 75 08.
www.theredwheelbarrow.com.
Métro: St Paul.

Books in English are available from:

Brentano's
37 avenue de l'Opéra. Tel: 01 42 61 52 50. Métro: Opéra.

Galignani
A well-stocked, old-fashioned bookshop, with bilingual service.
224 rue de Rivoli. Tel: 01 42 60 76 07. Métro: Concorde.

San Francisco Book Co
17 rue Monsieur-le-Prince. Tel: 01 43 29 15 70. Métro: Odéon. RER: Luxembourg.

WHSmith
248 rue de Rivoli. Tel: 01 44 77 88 99. Métro: Concorde.

Clothes

Apart from the exclusive fashion designers in the 8th *arrondissement*, there are trendy fashion boutiques in the area round St-Germain-des-Prés. Department stores have a choice of more traditional wear, while the Marais is ideal for discovering up-and-coming designers. Bargains can be found in the avenue de Clichy in the 17th *arrondissement*.

Gifts

Replicas from museum exhibits and objects by famous manufacturers are sold in four boutiques of the Association Paris-Musées:

Carnavalet
23 rue de Sévigné, 75003. Métro: St-Paul.

Forum des Halles
Rue Pierre Lescot. Métro: Les Halles.

Galliéra
10 avenue Pierre I de Serbie, 75016. Métro: Iéna.
(*See also* **Les Bouquinistes**, *p118.*)

Le Louvre
Métro: Palais-Royal.

Jewellery

From Boucheron to Cartier to Mauboussin, Paris has jewellery for every taste. Just venture into the area around place Vendome (home to top jewellers **Boucheron**, **Cartier** and **Van Cleef & Arpels**), to the splendid Champs-Elysées, or, for smaller boutiques, explore the streets around St Germain.

For fashion jewellery head to **Le Printemps**, the **Galeries Lafayette** (*see p142*) and the **Galerie Vivienne** (*see p77*).

Leather goods

Rue Tronchet, rue St-Lazare and adjacent streets (*métro: St-Lazare*), boulevard St-Michel and nearby (*métro: St-Michel*), and rue des Archives, Marais (*métro: Hôtel de Ville*).

Music

Three superstores compete to offer the best prices and a vast choice:

FNAC
Forum des Halles, 1 rue Pierre Lescot. Tel: 08 25 02 00 20. Métro: Les Halles.

FNAC Étoile
26 avenue des Ternes. Tel: 08 25 02 00 20. Métro: Ternes.

Virgin Megastore
52–60 avenue des Champs-Élysées. Tel: 01 49 53 50 00. Métro: Franklin-Roosevelt.

Fashion

While Paris is certainly known for being the home of brands such as YSL and Chanel, it seems that in the past years the true soul of Parisian fashion is to be found far from the big names and the boulevards. More and more fashion trends seem to come from the narrow streets of the Marais, or the once unpopular area along the Canal St Martin. Today the Parisian style is equally recognisable in a middle-aged woman elegantly dressed in designer clothes and in a crowd of hipsters having a coffee or a drink in one of the many cafés around rue des Archives.

For most people Paris fashion suggests a dreamworld of elegance, refinement, fantasy and originality that has helped create the glamorous image of the French capital.

Only a few designers and creators belong to the exclusive club of *haute couture* whose very existence depends on the collections. These are feverishly prepared in great secrecy and revealed during ritual fashion shows, in January and June for *haute couture*, March and October for *prêt-à-porter* (ready-to-wear). The media plays an essential role in these sophisticated 'performances', in which the top models are the stars. The designers create made-to-measure, very expensive outfits for a mainly foreign clientele. Behind the scenes a whole army of *petites mains* (seamstresses), embroiderers, milliners and so on works endless hours to realise the masterpieces. The creators, on the other hand, concentrate their efforts on *prêt-à-porter*, accessories and perfumes, initiating new styles and trends that are copied by clothes manufacturers everywhere.

To appreciate fully the important role played by Paris in the fashion world, and its real sense of beauty, take a walk in the Jardin des Tuileries around the time of Fashion Week. You'll see models, photographers, fashion editors and fashionista in their best looks. Whatever you see here is sure to be in the shops next season.

Well apart from the glittering world of designer clothes, the Sentier district (*rue Réaumur and side streets, métro Sentier*) houses a thousand or so stylists who are in direct contact with retail shops, and who test a limited number of designs. They then mass-produce the most successful ones in the space of a few days.

Major projects are under consideration to consolidate the success of the lucrative but vulnerable fashion industry. A *Maison de la mode* (headquarters of fashion) has been built under place du Carrousel at the Louvre, and there are plans for a *Cité internationale de la mode* near La Villette. However, above all, several specialised schools ensure that the young designers of tomorrow are being trained to follow in the footsteps of Cardin, Givenchy, Yves Saint Laurent, Christian Dior, Chanel, and a score of other household names that, despite repeated offensives from Milan, New York, London and Tokyo, have maintained Paris as the uncontested world capital of fashion.

Kenzo is a chain of stores selling clothes and perfumes

Entertainment

Monuments and museums are not the only form of entertainment for visitors to Paris. Opportunities for amusement and things to do abound – whether cultural or not, for the whole family or for adults only, by day or by night. Music lovers, opera buffs, cinephiles and simply those looking to have a good time are all very well catered for.

What's on

The Office du Tourisme et des Congrès de Paris brings out two publications: an annual one called *Saisons de Paris*, which lists the main events, and the more detailed monthly, *Paris Sélection*, which has a special section devoted to young people.

You can also ring **Paris Sélection Loisirs** (*tel: 08 92 68 30 00*) at any time of day or night to get pre-recorded weekly information in English. **Cultival** is a good booking agency, worth checking for suggestions and recommendations of cultural outings and events. *33 rue Le Peletier, 75009. Tel: 08 25 05 44 05. www.cultival.fr/en.*

Furthermore, there are two excellent weekly publications in French (both out on Wednesday): *Pariscope* and *L'Officiel des Spectacles.* They include up-to-date admission charges, and a special listing of restaurants open after midnight and on Sundays.

Tickets

Tickets for the theatre, concerts and other shows can be obtained directly from box offices or from the agencies listed below, through whom advance bookings can be made from abroad. This is strongly recommended as performances can become booked up very quickly.

Agence Perrosier, *6 place de la Madeleine, 75008. Tel: 01 42 60 58 31; fax: 01 42 60 14 83. Métro: Madeleine.*

FNAC Billeterie, all over Paris. *Tel: 08 92 68 36 22.*

Virgin Megastore, *52–60 Champs-Élysées, 75008. Tel: 01 49 53 50 08. Métro: Franklin-Roosevelt.*

Half-price tickets for performances the same day are available from the following kiosks (*open: Tue–Sat 12.30–7.45pm, Sun 12.30–4pm*): *15 place de la Madeleine, 75008. Métro: Madeleine; Esplanade de la Tour Montparnasse, 75015. Métro: Montparnasse-Bienvenue.*

Cinemas

Cinemas are a popular form of entertainment in Paris, and there is always a good choice of new releases, called *exclusivités*, and of old films, called *reprises*, often shown *en version originale* – *V.O.* for short (meaning in the original language) – particularly on the Champs-Élysées, in the Latin Quarter, in the Odéon district and at the complex at Bercy Village.

Some cinemas go in for festivals devoted to famous directors or actors. Classics are shown in the *cinémathèques* of the Palais de Chaillot and Palais de Tokyo, and in the Centre Pompidou, while the *vidéothèque* of the Forum des Halles mainly shows documentaries.

In most cinemas prices are reduced on Mondays. On other days children, students and sometimes senior citizens are entitled to a reduction.

Theatres

The most prestigious of them all, the **Comédie-Française**, also called Le Théâtre Français or simply Le Français (*1 place de la Comédie Française, 75001; tel: 01 44 58 15 15; métro: Palais-Royal. Also see p40*), traditionally puts on the great French classical comedies and tragedies by Molière, Racine and other masters. Its repertoire also includes selected 20th-century French and foreign plays. The acting is usually superb. The following theatres put on good productions of modern French and foreign plays. Booking starts two weeks in advance.

L'Atelier
Place Charles Dullin, 75018.
Tel: 01 46 06 49 24. Métro: Anvers.

Cartoucherie (Théâtre du Soleil)
Route du Champ-des-Manoeuvres, 75012. Tel: 01 43 74 87 63.
Métro: Château de Vincennes, then shuttle service.

Comédie des Champs-Élysées
15 avenue Montaigne, 75008.
Tel: 01 53 23 99 19.
www.comediedeschampselysees.com.
Métro: Alma-Marceau.

Espace Marais
22 rue Beautreillis, 75004.
Tel: 01 48 04 91 55. Métro: St-Paul.

Huchette
Eugène Ionesco plays.
23 rue de la Huchette, 75005.
Tel: 01 43 26 38 99. Métro: St-Michel.

Lucernaire Centre National d'Art et d'Essai
53 rue Notre-Dame-des-Champs, 75006.
Tel: 01 45 44 57 34. Métro: Vavin.

Poche Montparnasse
75 boulevard de Montparnasse, 75006.
Tel: 01 45 48 91 97. Métro: Montparnasse-Bienvenue.

(*Cont. on p154*)

Le Champo, the well-loved Latin Quarter cinema

Café life

The French café is an institution: it is not a bar, that is not subtle enough; it is not a pub, that is not Latin enough; it is not a wine bar either, although it does sell wine. In a word, the French café is unique. Most visitors to France know that, and their faces light up at the thought of indulging an hour or two sitting on the crowded terrace of a café watching the world go by.

Cafés are busy all day. They open early in the morning in time to serve the traditional *grand crème* (large cup of white coffee) with croissants to people on their way to work. Throughout the day they serve wine by the glass, beer – *un demi* (originally ½ litre, just over a pint), or *une pression* (a glass of draught beer) – or *un pastis*, a strong aniseed drink diluted with water, and, of course, the tiny *espresso*, a cup of strong black coffee that seems to keep French people going. Drinks are cheaper *au bar* (standing at the bar) than *en salle* (sitting at one of the typical round tables). You can always spot the waiters and waitresses, wearing the traditional black and white uniform, as they make their way through the crowd with great agility.

The local cafés, where 'regulars' have their drink at 11am, working people eat a quick snack at lunchtime, and local residents meet in the evening to catch up on

No one does coffee quite like the French

the news, play an important role in the city's social life. They have nothing in common with the elegant establishments of place de l'Opéra, full of wealthy tourists and retired Parisians, or even with the Left Bank cafés where a fashionable elite goes to be seen.

The popularity of cafés is often linked to the fact that apartments in Paris are very small, so people tend to socialise more outside: in public parks when the sun is out, and in cafés during the colder months.

Following the economic downturn of 2009 many journalists reporting from Paris noticed a decrease in the number of people sitting at cafés. However, such a trend appears to have been short-lived. Either because VAT on restaurant and café bills dropped to 5.5 per cent from 19.6 per cent, or simply on account of France's improved economic situation, the French seem to have gone back to their cafés.

An interesting phenomenon that has taken place over the past few years is the increasing presence of foreign chains across the Parisian streets. Notwithstanding the well-known Parisian pride and the high costs of beverages from such chains, the various Starbucks cafés are always busy.

An old-fashioned café display

Theatre Hébertot
78 bis boulevard des Batignolles, 75017. Tel: 01 43 87 23 23. Métro: Villiers, Rome.

Théâtre National de Chaillot
1 place du Trocadéro, 75016. Tel: 01 53 65 30 00. Métro: Trocadéro.

Music

Classical concerts

Paris has many orchestras. The most prestigious are the Orchestre National de France, the Orchestre Philharmonique de Radio France, the Orchestre de Paris and the Ensemble Intercontemporain. The main venues vary in size from the small **Salle Gaveau** to the vast **Théâtre des Champs-Élysées** and the **Salle Pleyel**. There are lunchtime or early evening concerts in many churches throughout the capital, concerts in parks and gardens from May to September, and an enterprising operation, *Monuments en Musique*, which provides short musical programmes at regular intervals in selected monuments.

Opera and ballet

Most major operas are now staged at the **Opéra Bastille**, but the **Opéra Garnier** seems to be getting its share again, when technical conditions permit. The rest of the time it is the exclusive home of ballet.

Jazz, rock and pop music

Concerts are usually held in large venues such as the **Zénith** at La Villette

(*see p103*), the **Palais Omnisports Paris-Bercy** (*boulevard de Bercy, 75012; métro: Bercy*) and the **Palais des Congrès** (*Porte Maillot, 75017; métro: Porte Maillot*). The old **Olympia** music hall (*boulevard des Capucines, 75009; métro: Opéra*) is the traditional venue for variety shows.

Nightlife

Like most capital cities, Paris has a large number of bars, discos, nightclubs and sex shows (the latter mainly in the sleazy Pigalle area), but its **cabaret** shows are still considered the most typically French form of night entertainment. They became famous at the turn of the 20th century, partly for their lavish, colourful productions and partly because they shocked the predominantly bourgeois society. Today they no longer shock, but the productions are just as lavish.

The famous Moulin Rouge

Crazy Horse Saloon
Reputed to be the most erotic of all.
12 avenue George V, 75008.
Tel: 01 47 23 32 32.
www.lecrazyhorseparis.com.
Métro: George V.

Folies Bergères
32 rue Richer, 75009. Tel: 01 44 79 98 90.
www.foliesbergere.com.
Métro: Grands Boulevards or Cadet.

Lido
Very sophisticated light effects.
116 bis avenue des Champs-Élysées,
75008. Tel: 01 40 76 56 10. www.lido.fr.
Métro: George V.

Moulin Rouge
The most famous, with its 'girls'
dancing the French cancan.
82 boulevard de Clichy, 75018.
Tel: 01 53 09 82 82.
www.moulinrouge.fr.
Métro: Blanche.

Jazz clubs
Very popular, also very crowded; arrive
early but don't expect things to get
going before 11pm.

Au Duc des Lombards
Small, cosy club.
42 rue des Lombards, 75001.
Tel: 01 42 33 22 88.
www.ducdeslombards.com.
Métro: Châtelet-les-Halles.

Caveau de la Huchette
Authentic jazz cellar with dancing (rock
'n' roll) to live bands.
5 rue de la Huchette, 75005.
Tel: 01 43 26 65 05.
Métro: St-Michel.

La Villa
Chic and cosy jazz club in small St-
Germain-des-Prés hotel.
29 rue Jacob, 75006.
Tel: 01 43 26 60 00.
www.villa-saintgermain.com.
Métro: St-Germain-des-Prés.

New Morning
Jazz and world music venue
featuring internationally
acclaimed musicians.
7–9 rue des Petites Écuries, 75010.
Tel: 01 45 23 51 41.
Métro: Château d'eau.

Petit Journal Montparnasse
Blues, African and traditional jazz.
80 avenue Maine, Mouchotte, 75014.
Tel: 01 43 21 56 70.
Métro: Gaîté.

Nightclubs
These liven up from midnight onwards.

Favela Chic Paris
A fusion of Brazilian and French style
in this restaurant that turns into a hip
club after midnight.
18 rue du Faubourg du Temple, 75011.
Tel: 01 40 21 38 14.
www.favelachic.com

La Loco
Trendy nightclub near Montmartre.
90 boulevard de Clichy, 75018.
Tel: 01 53 41 88 88.
Métro: Blanche.

La Scala
Special effects with laser lights.
188 bis rue de Rivoli, 75001.
Tel: 01 42 61 64 00.
Métro: Palais-Royal or Tuileries.

Children

Paris and the Île-de-France offer children of all ages a choice of entertaining activities, whatever the weather. Head for Paris's parks in summer, where children can make the most of the fine weather with various oudoor pursuits. In winter take advantage of the outdoor ice-skating rinks set in major locations such as Montparnasse tower and at Place de l'Hôtel de Ville. A climb up the Tour Eiffel will thrill youngsters of all ages, while older ones will enjoy the Conciergerie and its gruesome stories, the Château de Vincennes and Versailles.

From the skies
Paris Air Balloon
If you are keen on seeing Paris from a different point of view, head towards the *15th arrondissement*. Here, in the Parc André Citroën, grown ups and children can go up on the aerostat. *www.ballondeparis.com. Admission charge. Métro: Javel or Balard.*

Museums
The **Musée Grévin** in the boulevard Montmartre, with its wax figures of famous historical and contemporary characters, is both entertaining and educational (*see p80*).

The **Cité des Sciences et de l'Industrie** at La Villette (*see pp102–3*) offers an introduction to science and technology called **Cité des Enfants** with interactive workshops.

The **Centre Georges Pompidou** (*see pp22–5*) aims to help children discover art through workshops.

The **Louvre** (*see pp37–40*) has many workshops and tours aimed at children.

The **Palais de la Découverte** (*see p66*) has fascinating and easy-to-understand science exhibitions and interactive demonstrations.

The world of the sea
Aquarium Tropical
See pp104–5.
L'Argonaute
A real submarine and an exhibition at the Cité des Sciences et de l'Industrie.
Centre de la Mer et des Eaux
At this marine and freshwater centre, simple phenomena are explained through observation, games and audio-visual presentations.
195 rue St-Jacques, 75005. Tel: 01 44 32 10 70. www.oceano.org. Open: Tue–Fri 10am–12.30pm & 1.30–5.30pm, Sat–Sun 10am–5.30pm. Closed: Mon, and Sat–Sun in Aug. Admission charge. Métro: Luxembourg.
Cineaqua
France's new aquarium mixes multi-media with fish tanks, presenting over 500 species of aquatic life. There are

157

three cinemas, live shows, workshops and a fish 'petting' pool.

Palais Chaillot in the Trocadéro gardens. 5 Avenue Albert De Mun, 75016. Tel: 01 40 69 23 23. www.cineaqua.com. Open: daily 10am–7pm. Admission charge. Metro: Trocadéro.

Parks and gardens
Jardin d'Acclimatation
A little train dating from 1878 runs a shuttle service between the Porte Maillot station and the park every 20 minutes or so from 10.15am. Other attractions include an enchanted house, miniature golf and a puppet theatre.

Bois de Boulogne, 75016. Tel: 01 40 67 90 82. www.jardindacclimatation.fr. Open: daily 10am–6pm (winter); 10am–7pm (summer). Admission charge. Métro: Porte Maillot (little train) or Sablons.

Jardin du Luxembourg
Adventure playgrounds, puppet shows and toy wooden yachts for hire to sail on the central pond.

Rue de Médicis, 75005. RER: Luxembourg.

While most parks in the capital have a children's play area, three are better equipped: the **Parc des Buttes-Chaumont** (*see p105*), the **Parc Georges Brassens** (*see p122*) and the **Parc Floral de Paris** in the Bois de Vincennes (*see p101*).

Zoos
There is a small zoo in the **Jardin des Plantes** (*see p59*) and another in the **Bois de Vincennes** (*see p101*).

The perfect mixture: kids and open space

Children

Fun with water
Aquaboulevard
An aquatic adventure playground. It offers attractions such as giant slides and a bubble pool.

4 rue Louis Armand, 75015. Tel: 01 40 60 10 00. Open: Mon–Thur 9am–11pm, Fri–Sat 9am–midnight, Sun 8am–11pm. Admission charge. Métro: Balard.

In fine weather children will enjoy a boat trip on the **Lac Inférieur** in the Bois de Boulogne or on the **Lac Daumesnil** in the Bois de Vincennes, and also a trip on the Seine in one of the **Bateaux Mouches** boats (*see p184*).

Shows
There are *Guignol* (Punch and Judy) shows in most public parks and gardens. Paris also has a number of circuses that move about according to the season: the **Cirque d'Hiver Bouglione** (*tel: 01 47 00 28 81*), **Cirque Bormann** (*tel: 01 64 05 36 25*) and **Cirque Gruss** (*tel: 03 22 91 79 32. www.cirque-gruss.com*).

Sport and leisure

Regular television coverage of sports events has contributed to a change of attitude towards sport in France, and particularly in Paris. Sport has entered every home, and the number of spectators has reached phenomenal proportions. As a result, more money has been invested in making sport accessible to a wider public. Stadiums and large indoor venues have been modernised, and facilities for individual sports have improved.

SPORTS CENTRES AND STADIUMS

Built in 1984, **Palais Omnisports Paris-Bercy** is a huge, multi-purpose centre with a seating capacity of 17,000. There is also an ice-skating rink. It is also frequently used for rock concerts (*8 boulevard de Bercy, 75012; tel: 08 92 39 01 00; www.bercy.fr; métro: Bercy*).

Opened in 1998 with a capacity of 80,000 spectators, the **Stade de France** is the main venue for international football and rugby matches (*Zac du Cornillon Nord, Saint-Denis 93216; tel: 08 92 70 09 00; www.stadefrance.com; métro: Saint-Denis – Porte de Paris*).

The **Parc des Princes** is home to Paris Saint-Germain FC (*24 rue du Commandant-Guilbaud, 75016; www.leparcdesprinces.fr; métro: Exelmans or Porte de St-Cloud*).

Quite close is the famous **Stade Roland Garros**, which stages the annual French Open tennis competition. The tennis complex has 16 courts, including a centre court with room for 16,500 spectators (*2 avenue Gordon Bennett,* *75016; tel: 01 47 43 48 00; www.rolandgarros.com; métro: Porte d'Auteuil*).

Next to it, on the edge of the Bois de Boulogne, are two of Paris's three racecourses: the **Hippodrome d'Auteuil** (*champs de course d'Auteuil; tel: 01 40 71 47 47; métro: Porte d'Auteuil*) and the **Hippodrome de Longchamp** (*route des Tribunes, Bois de Boulogne, 75116; tel: 01 44 30 75 00; métro: Porte d'Auteuil, then shuttle bus*). The third racecourse is the **Hippodrome de Vincennes** on the other side of town (*2 route de la Ferme, 75012; tel: 01 49 77 17 17; RER: Joinville-le-Pont; métro: Château de Vincennes*).

In the 16th *arrondissement*, the **Stade Pierre de Coubertin** stages events such as judo and fencing competitions, gymnastics and dance displays, boxing and basketball matches (*82 avenue Georges Lafont, 75016; tel: 01 45 27 79 12; métro: Porte de St-Cloud*).

The **Stade Georges Carpentier** holds indoor sports competitions such as martial arts, volleyball, badminton and table tennis (*81 boulevard Masséna, 75013; tel: 01 45 85 57 43; métro: Porte d'Ivry or Porte de Choisy*).

The vast new **Stade Charléty**, with a capacity of 20,000 spectators, hosts both outdoor and indoor sports, from football to athletics and tennis (*87 blvd Kellerman, 75013; tel: 01 44 16 00 00; métro: Cité Universitaire*).

Built for the 1924 Olympic Games, the **Piscine Georges Vallerey** (swimming pool) was modernised in 1989 and can now hold water polo events, as well as international swimming competitions (*148 avenue Gambetta, 75020; tel: 01 58 05 02 30; métro: Porte des Lilas*).

SPECTATOR SPORTS
Cycling
The colourful and often dramatic finish of the Tour de France is staged along the Champs-Élysées.

Football
The final of the Coupe de France is usually held in Paris in April or May.

Horse racing
On the south side of the Bois de Boulogne, Auteuil specialises in steeplechasing and is famous for its difficult jumps, while flat racing takes place at Longchamp. Prestigious races include the Prix du Président de la République, which takes place on Palm Sunday, and the Grand Prix de l'Arc de Triomphe on the first Sunday in October. The Vincennes racecourse is popular for trotting events.

Rugby
France's home games in the Six Nations Tournament are held at the Stade de France.

Running
The famous Marathon de Paris takes place in the capital in March or April.

Tennis
The Championnats Internationaux de France (French Open) take place at the Stade Roland Garros in late May and early June. The Open de la Ville de Paris is held in the Palais Omnisports de Paris-Bercy in late October.

PARTICIPATORY SPORTS
There are more than 250 locations all over Paris where amateurs and professionals can practise the sport of their choice. Municipal equipment is available to everyone for a very modest fee, and visitors are able to join certain private clubs on a temporary basis.

To get the best information on what is available in your area, contact the Office Municipal des Sports in the *mairie d'arrondissement* (district town hall). You can also obtain from the town hall a booklet entitled *Centre d'Animation Magazine*, published twice yearly, which contains a list of all sports centres, with addresses and programmes. *Sport à la carte* has been specially devised to provide individual programmes in municipal centres at fixed hours.

Climbing

Three new structures have been installed in the city to accommodate the growing number of enthusiasts; the most impressive is located at the **Stade des Poissonniers**, *2 rue Jean Cocteau, 75018. Tel: 01 42 51 24 68. Open: Mon–Sat 7.30am–10pm, Sun 8am–6pm. Maximum height: 21m (70 ft). Métro: Porte de Clignancourt.*

For other possibilities and information contact the **Fédération Française de la Montagne et de l'Escalade** (*8–10 quai de la Marne, 75019; tel: 01 40 18 75 50; www.ffme.fr*).

Cycling

Nearly 400 clubs in the Paris region organise tours in Île-de-France. For information contact:
Fédération Française de Cyclisme
5 rue de Rome, 75008.
Tel: 01 49 35 69 00; www.ffc.fr

Golf

Several clubs and centres offer golfers the possibility of practising putting, and even their drive, with the help of simulators. However, the real thing takes place out of town. For detailed information contact:
Fédération Française de Golf
68 Anatole France, Levallois-Perret,
92300. Tel: 01 41 49 77 00;
www.ffgolf.org

Rollerblading

Every weekend Paris is taken over by rollerblades. On Sundays, starting at 2.30pm from Place de la Bastille, families and skaters of all ability levels, including beginners, are welcome. On Fridays, starting at 9.30pm from Place Raoul-Dautry, experienced skaters gather for a night ride.
www.pari-roller.com.
www.rollers-coquillages.org

Swimming

There are many municipal swimming pools in Paris as well as a number of private ones. These are the most attractive:

Piscine des Halles
An Olympic-size pool with a view of the tropical glasshouse.
Forum des Halles. Level 3.
Tel: 01 42 36 98 44;
www.nageurs.com.
Métro: Les Halles.

Piscine Jean Taris
Lovely Japanese garden setting.
16 rue Thouin, 75005. Tel: 01 55 42 81 90.
Métro: Cardinal-Lemoine.

Piscine Josephine Baker
A spectacular floating pool on the Seine, in the modern Port de la Gare area, right by the new National Library.
Port de la Gare, quai François Mauriac, 75013. Tel: 01 56 61 96 50. Métro: Bibliothèque François Mitterrand.

Piscine Pontoise
19 rue de Pontoise, 75005.
Tel: 01 55 42 77 88.
Métro: Maubert-Mutualité.

Tennis and squash

There are 150 municipal tennis courts
open until 10pm, at very reasonable fees.
For detailed information, contact the
local town hall or Allo-Sports (*see p188*).
There are also several private clubs:

Squash Montmartre
Four courts, clubhouse, restaurant.
14 rue Achille Martinet, 75018.
Tel: 01 42 55 38 30.
Métro: Lamarck.

Squash Rennes Raspail
Seven courts and golf practice.
149 rue de Rennes, 75006.
Tel: 01 45 44 24 35. Métro: Rennes.

Tennis de Longchamp
Twenty courts.
19 boulevard Anatole-France, 92
Boulogne. Tel: 01 48 25 41 26.
Métro: Porte d'Auteuil.

Tenpin bowling

This has been popular with young
people for some time, more as a leisure
activity than a sport.

Bowling Foch
2 bis avenue Foch, 75016.
Tel: 01 45 00 00 13. Open: daily
11am–2am. Bar. Métro: Étoile.

Bowling Montparnasse
27 rue Commandant René Mouchotte,
75014. Tel: 01 43 21 61 32. Open: daily
10am–2am (4am on Fri & Sat).
Bar-restaurant. Métro: Montparnasse.

Bowling Nord-Ouest de Paris-Champerret
1 rue Caporal Peugeot, 75017.
Tel: 01 43 80 24 64.
Open: daily 10am–2am. Bar.
Métro: Porte de Champerret.

Watersports

Kayaking and canoeing are possible at
the **Bassin de la Villette**, *41 bis quai de
la Loire, 75019; Tel: 01 42 40 29 90;
métro: Jaurès or Stalingrad.*

Leisure parks outside Paris

Activities include swimming, sailing,
windsurfing, riding and tennis.

Base de Loisirs, Torcy, Seine-et-Marne,
route de Lagny *77200 Torcy. 25km
(15^1/$_2$ miles) east of Paris.
Tel: 01 60 20 02 04. Open: 9am–6pm.
RER: Torcy.*

Le Val de Seine
*Chemin du Rouillard, 78480 Verneuil-
sur-Seine. 30km (18 miles) west of Paris.
Tel: 01 39 28 16 20. Open: daily
9am–noon, 2–6pm.*

Boules in the Bois de Vincennes

Food and drink

Food is an important ingredient of the French way of life and some of the rituals that accompany its preparation and consumption are still performed by a majority of French people, even in Paris where the pressures of modern city life seem to go against the more traditional principles of gastronomy.

Eating out

The choice is vast and each type of establishment has its own personality. Crowded at lunchtime, cafés are ideal for a quick meal, with a restricted menu usually consisting of *steak/frites* (steak and chips), mixed salads and a selection of sandwiches made with crisp *baguettes* (French bread). Slightly more expensive, *brasseries* offer a choice of traditional dishes that include an Alsatian *choucroute garnie* (sauerkraut with assorted sausages). Top *brasseries* have an attractive display of fresh seafood just outside their premises. There are several such establishments on place de Clichy, not far from the Moulin Rouge.

Wine bars are becoming increasingly popular as a lunchtime venue. They serve an assortment of cold platters and cheese with selected wines by the glass. **L'Écluse** (*15 quai des Grands Augustins, 75006; métro: St-Michel*) is one of the most famous, and a good place to sample for atmosphere.

Little known or talked about are the discreet but charming *salons de thé* (tearooms), often tucked away in picturesque streets and passages. They offer the luxury of a relaxed atmosphere in refined surroundings, and serve good-quality snacks and pastries with a choice of fine teas or coffee. Two of the best are **Mariage Frères** (*35 rue du Bourg-Tibourg in the Marais*) and **La Cour de Rohan** (*Cour du Commerce St-André, 59–61 rue St-André-des-Arts, near place St-Michel*).

The name 'restaurant' applies to a wide range of establishments, from the unassuming, friendly, local place, to the select, fashionable, outrageously expensive rendezvous for gourmets. The variety stems from the type of cuisine served. Typical cuisines from the regions of France are well represented and in some cases they are concentrated in a specific area. For instance, exponents of Breton cuisine are grouped in the vicinity of the Gare

Montparnasse, while specialities from the Auvergne are to be found in the Bastille area.

The number of ethnic restaurants has increased lately and they, too, tend to congregate in specific areas, sometimes taking over a whole street, like rue de la Huchette, near place St-Michel, which is lined with cheap Greek and North African restaurants. Rue des Rosiers and adjacent streets in the Marais are well known for their Jewish and East European restaurants. The 13th *arrondissement*, near Porte d'Ivry, where Asian restaurants are plentiful, has been christened 'Chinatown'. By contrast, you hardly notice the less conspicuous presence of several Japanese restaurants in the Opéra district.

Vegetarian food

Vegetarians may struggle a little in Paris as French cuisine is very strongly meat-based. Although vegetarianism is regarded as a kind of eccentricity, almost everywhere will have a range of salads and maybe pasta dishes – but watch out for salads with bacon in them!

The price range given in the listings below refers to an average meal per person, not including drinks. There are four categories:

£	Less than €30
££	€30–45
£££	€45–75
££££	More than €75

(*Cont. on p166*)

Food and drink

Mixed salad: a range of fresh produce is on offer

Cuisine

It is a well-known, although controversial, fact that 'Paris is not France'; the French themselves acknowledge it, especially if they are not Parisians. Yet, paradoxically, although there is no Parisian cuisine as such, Paris has become a melting pot of the best culinary traditions, and the undisputed capital of French gastronomy.

The French are particular about 'fresh' food: bread, meat and vegetables are usually bought daily. A lot of people shop after working hours, which explains why food shops and markets stay open late.

Baguettes: the iconic French bread

Although two main meals a day is usual, around midday and 8pm, in Paris lunch tends to be reduced to a quick light meal, the emphasis being on the evening meal served with wine. Breakfast is not very copious: freshly bought bread with butter and jam, marmalade or honey, and/or a croissant. *Boulangeries* open early so people can drop in for fresh supplies before going to work.

Variety is the first and foremost characteristic of French cuisine. The ingredients used in cooking have regional origins: cream, butter and cheese are widely used in northern areas where milk products are plentiful, while olive oil and garlic are typical of Mediterranean areas, and red wine makes casseroles rich and tasty in the Bourgogne district.

The universal fame of traditional French cuisine rests on the variety of its regional dishes.

Among starters you may find *hors-d'oeuvre variés* (raw vegetables seasoned with oil and vinegar, served with assorted *charcuterie*), *quiche lorraine* (savoury flan with pieces of bacon), *moules marinières* (mussels simmered in white wine with

France boasts more than 500 different cheeses

shallots) or the delicious *soupe à l'onion grâtinée* (onion soup with melted cheese).

Main dishes usually include several of the following: *entrecôte bordelaise* (juicy steak with a rich wine sauce), *boeuf bourguignon* (casseroled beef with onions and mushrooms, in a red Burgundy wine), *blanquette de veau* (stewed veal with cream and mushrooms) and *choucroute garnie* (sauerkraut cooked in dry white wine, with pork and sausages). *Gratin dauphinois* (sliced potatoes baked with cream and grated cheese) is ideal with tasty grills.

To finish a good meal there is nothing more refreshing than a home-baked *crème caramel* (egg custard coated with caramel), or a cool *baba-au-rhum* (light sponge cake with rum syrup).

However, French cuisine does not rely for its success on tradition alone, for it is constantly being reinvented and perfected by ambitious young chefs whose imagination has no bounds.

Food and drink

THE HISTORIC CENTRE
Beaubourg, Forum des Halles

Au Pied de Cochon £
An old classic. Serves traditional onion soup and pigs' trotters.
6 rue Coquillière, 75001. Tel: 01 40 13 77 00. Métro: Les Halles.

Le Rocher de Cancale £
Loved by locals and visitors alike. Enjoy your dishes while sitting on the terrace – perfect for people-watching – or in the upstairs rooms.
78 rue Montorgueil, 75002. Tel: 01 42 33 50 29. Métro: Les Halles or Sentier.

Silk & Spice ££
Chef Siripark Nopporn works wonders with his sophisticated Thai dishes.
6 rue Mandar, 75002. Tel: 01 44 88 21 91. Métro: Bourse or Sentier.

L'Escargot £££
If you only sample escargot once during your trip to Paris, do it at this upmarket restaurant. They also offer a lunch menu and a selection of other dishes.
38 rue Montorgueil, 75002. Tel: 01 42 36 83 51. Métro: Étienne Marcel.

Marais
Breakfast in America ££
If you fancy something other than French food, this restaurant offers a selection of burgers and pancakes.
4 rue Malher, 75004. Tel: 01 42 72 40 21. Métro: Saint-Paul.

Vin des Pyrénées ££
Informal setting and cosy atmosphere in this restaurant that offers food with a Pyrénées flavour.
25 rue Beautreillis, 75004. Tel: 01 42 72 64 94. Métro: Bastille.

Louvre and Rivoli
Aux Lyonnais ££
Lyon cooking Alain Ducasse-style has locals flocking to this restaurant.
32 rue St-Marc, 75002. Tel: 01 42 96 65 04. Métro: Richelieu Drouot.

Chez Pierre au Palais Royal ££
Come here to savour the inventive cuisine of chef Pascal Bataillé: the *boudin noir* (blood sausage) is a revelation, as are the more unusual wasabi vegetables and ginger sorbet.
10 rue de Richelieu, 75001. Tel: 01 42 96 09 17. Métro: Palais-Royal.

Le Taste Monde ££
A restaurant that pairs delicious French food with a world tour of wine.
8 rue de Surène, 75008. Tel: 01 42 66 19 89. Métro: Madeleine or Concorde.

Île de la Cité
Le Pamphlet ££
Affordable sophistication in this fashionable restaurant. Book ahead to sample the inventive modern cuisine.
38 rue Debelleyme, Île St-Louis 75003. Tel: 01 42 72 39 24. Métro: Filles du Calvaire.

Quartier Latin
AOC ££
An archetypal Paris bistro. The *entrecôte* makes it heaven for carnivores.
14 rue des Fossés St-Bernard, 75005. Tel: 01 43 54 22 52. Métro: Cardinal Lemoine. www.restoaoc.com

Mavrommatis ££
This small, friendly Greek cantina has the city's best Greek food with lots of fresh cod and squid.

42 rue Daubenton, 75005.
Tel: 01 43 31 17 17.
Métro: Monge.

L'Atelier de Maître Albert £££
Fixed-price menu includes half a bottle of wine.
1 rue Maître Albert, 75005.
Tel: 01 56 81 30 01.
Métro: Maubert-Mutualité.

La Tour d'Argent ££££
Expensive, excellent food.
15 quai de la Tournelle, 75005. Tel: 01 40 46 71 11.
Métro: Maubert-Mutualité.

St-Germain-des-Prés

Aux Charpentiers £
Publishers' haunt.
10 rue Mabillon, 75006.
Tel: 01 43 26 30 05.
Métro: Mabillon.

Le Petit Saint Benoît £
Charming restaurant serving unpretentious home-cooked food.
4 rue Saint-Benoît, 75006.
Tel: 01 42 60 27 92. Métro:
St-Germain-des-Prés.

Polidor £
Authentic bistro with convivial atmosphere.
41 rue Monsieur-le-Prince, 75006.
Tel: 01 43 26 95 34.
Métro: Odéon.

Le Petit Zinc ££
Typical bistro serving excellent seafood.

11 rue Saint-Benoît,
75006. Tel: 01 42 86 61 00.
Métro: St-Germain-des-Prés.

Les Bouquinistes £££
Fashionable restaurant along the embankment.
53 quai des Grands Augustins, 75006.
Tel: 01 43 25 45 94.
Métro: St-Michel.

Helene D'Arroze £££
Michelin star-winner Helene D'Arroze prepares incredible dishes reinventing traditional recipes. The

upstairs area is more formal and expensive, while the downstairs bistro is more relaxed.
4 rue d'Assas, 75006.
Tel: 01 42 22 00 11.
Métro: Rennes.

NORTH AND WEST OF THE HISTORIC CENTRE
Arc de Triomphe
Bar à Huîtres Ternes ££
A bustling, democratic bistro for eager eaters of oysters and all things fresh and fishy.

A typical bistro in Montmartre

Food and drink

69 avenue de Wagram,
75017.
Tel: 01 43 80 63 54.
Métro: Ternes.

**Le Bistrot d'à Côté
Flaubert ££**
New chef-owner has
transformed this food
shop into a fine bistro.
10 rue Gustave Flaubert,
75017. Tel: 01 42 67 05 81.
Métro: Courcelles.

SYDR ££
Owned in partnership by
celebrity chef Alain
Dutournier and former
French national team
rugby captain Philippe
Sella. They have created a
designer, gourmet
version of the rowdy
sports bar.
6 rue de Tilsitt, 75008.
Tel: 01 45 72 41 32.
Métro: Étoile.

**Atelier des
Compères £££**
A small gourmet outpost
hidden in a courtyard.
Sommelier Jacques
Boudin will discover the
perfect wine for each dish.
56 rue Galilée, 75008.
Tel: 01 47 20 75 56.
Métro: Étoile.

Le Boeuf sur le Toit £££
Famous Art Deco
brasserie with a lovely
atmosphere.

34 rue du Colisée, 75008.
Tel: 01 53 93 65 55.
Métro: Saint-Philippe du
Roule or Franklin D
Roosevelt.

Taillevent ££££
High-class cuisine. Book
months ahead.
15 rue Lamennais, 75008.
Tel: 01 44 95 15 01.
Métro: George V.

Tour Eiffel and Trocadéro

Le Petit Rétro £
Suberb traditional
cuisine served in a
listed building with
1910 décor.
5 rue Mesnil, 75016.
Tel: 01 44 05 06 05.
Métro: Victor Hugo.

L'Astrance ££
A first-rate bistro with
contemporary décor.
4 rue Beethoven, 75006.
Tel: 01 40 50 84 40.
Métro: Passy.

La Butte Chaillot ££
Refined cuisine; striking
contemporary setting.
110 bis avenue Kléber,
75016. Tel: 01 47 27 88
88. Métro: Trocadéro.

**Alain Ducasse au Plaza
Athénée ££££**
Futuristic design.
Inspired cuisine by a
great chef.

21 avenue Montaigne,
75008. Tel: 01 53 67 65 00.
Métro: Alma-Marceau.

Grands Boulevards

Chartier £
Chartier is so old-
fashioned it's now
fashionably retro. Steak
frites and other plain
grub in a workmanlike
fin-de-siècle setting.
7 rue du Faubourg
Montmartre, 75009.
Tel: 01 47 70 86 29.
Métro: Grands Boulevards.

Montmartre

Le Moulin à Vins £
Lively and rustic with
succulent charcuterie.
6 rue Burq, 75008.
Tel: 01 42 52 81 27.
Métro: Abbesses.

Pétrelle £
If you'll eat anything
then Pétrelle's no-choice
menu is a terrific deal,
and you'll soon taste
why the place has
become a fashionable
hang-out.
34 rue Pétrelle, 75009.
Tel: 01 42 82 11 02.
Métro: Anvers.

L'Étrier ££
Refined, traditional
French cuisine; good
value. Book ahead.

154 rue Lamarck, 75018.
Tel: 01 42 29 14 01.
Métro: Guy Moquet.

Des Si & des Mets ££
Great option for gluten-intolerant travellers. This restaurant offers a range of delicious dishes catering to coeliacs.
63 rue Lepic, 75018.
Tel: 01 42 55 19 61.
www.dessietdesmets.com.
Métro: Abbesses.

Ozu £££
Some of the best sushi and monkfish in Paris is served in this building constructed for the 1878 World Exhibition but now revamped as the new CinéAqua aquarium.
5 Avenue Albert de Mun, 75116. Tel: 01 40 69 23 90. Métro: Trocadéro.

SOUTH OF THE HISTORIC CENTRE
Rive Gauche
La Petite Chaise £
Excellent value.
36 rue de Grenelle, 75007.

Tel: 01 42 22 13 35.
Métro: Sèvres-Babylone.

Chez Les Anges ££
This restaurant was much loved by President Mitterrand. The menu here is seasonal, from wild duck and venison to Norman lamb, shellfish and turbot.
54 Blvd de La Tour Maubourg, 75007.
Tel: 01 47 05 89 86.
Métro: La Tour Maubourg.

Food and drink

Cafés serve simple but tasty food

Wines

Wine is the French national drink, its infinite variety matching that of French cuisine. Vines have been grown in France since Roman times, and ancestral traditions are still observed in many regions. Wine-making methods are strictly controlled, and a grading system is applied accordingly.

Vin de table is a cheap, ordinary wine. It is drunk 'young' (within a year). *Vin délimité de qualité supérieure* (VDQS) is a higher-grade wine that is produced in areas where quality is constant. *Appellation d'Origine Contrôlée* (AOC) denotes a wine characteristic of a specific district, or *cru*, such as Médoc in the Bordeaux region.

This information and more is on the labels, which are well worth studying when selecting a good red or white château wine. Look for the year, as quality varies from year to year, and for the words *mis en bouteille au château* (bottled at the château); but bear in mind that there are many château wines and the best of them have been graded as *cru bourgeois* and *grand cru* or *1er cru*, *2ème cru*, and so on.

The two main wine-producing regions are the Bordeaux region in the southwest with famous wines such as Médoc, Graves, St-Émilion or Pomerol, and Bourgogne in the east, with inspiring names such as Nuits-St-Georges, Chambertin, Pommard and Pouilly-Fuissé.

However, other regions also produce some great wines: for instance, Châteauneuf-du-Pape, which comes from the Rhône Valley, and Riesling from the Alsace. Champagne, named after the region in northeastern France, is in a class of its own.

The lengthy production process was perfected in the 17th century by Dom Pérignon, a monk who came from the Abbaye d'Hautvillers.

Wine-bottle shapes vary from one region to another, providing an immediate clue to the origins of their contents. Thus, the elegant, slim bottle from the southwest contrasts with the stockier type used in the Bourgogne and Champagne regions, or the tall fluted ones typical of Alsace.

As culinary tourism is becoming more and more important, so too is wine tourism – a trend that Parisians seem to have accepted very quickly. While once wine shops were merely designed to sell wine, and were not always welcoming, now such venues can often be found hosting wine-tasting sessions and other events. From small *caves* to the wine cellars of large department stores such as Galeries Lafayette (*see p142*), buying wines in Paris has become a feast for the eyes, the palate and also the mind.

Whatever your taste, your budget or the occasion, there's a bottle of wine to suit it

Accommodation

Old and new, traditional and modern, Parisian hotels vary considerably in size and the degree of comfort they offer. During the last few years many have been renovated, modernised and refurbished, with the emphasis on proper separate bathroom facilities instead of the usual washbasin and bidet, even in the lowest grade. Only the more expensive hotels have restaurants.

Grading

Hotels are graded by the Direction de l'Industrie Touristique, according to the degree of comfort and quality of services:

- HT, HRT or 1-star applies to modest hotels with basic comforts.
- 2-star denotes a hotel in which you can expect a private bathroom.
- 3-star qualifies a very comfortable hotel, with private bathrooms and breakfast served in the rooms if you wish.
- 4-star is granted to high-class hotels, some of which are internationally famous.
- 5-star is granted to only a very few de luxe hotels that the French call *palaces*.

As they are in greater demand, there are more 2- and 3-star hotels throughout the city.

Breakfast

As a rule all hotels provide breakfast, but generally only 3-star and above offer room service. The price of breakfast is quoted separately from that of the room, and, though you are expected to, you are not obliged to have it.

A 'continental' breakfast usually includes tea, milk, coffee or chocolate, a baguette with butter and jam, and croissants. Some hotels now offer an English-style breakfast to guests on payment of a supplement.

Prices

By Western standards, Parisian hotels are fairly reasonably priced. Charging by the room rather than per person is still common practice (some hotels have family rooms for parents with one or two children).

Prices are not controlled, and so vary a lot according to the time of year, and from one hotel to another; they can also be changed without prior notice.

The easiest method of payment is by credit card, which only a few hotels in the lowest category do not accept.

Selecting a hotel

Staying in central areas keeps travelling times to a minimum and allows you to enjoy the atmosphere of the city to the full. In general, most luxury hotels are in the Madeleine, Opéra and Champs-Élysées area, which covers the 1st, 8th and 9th *arrondissements*, while the left bank, especially the 5th, 6th and 7th, has a profusion of smaller, more relaxed, but still very comfortable establishments.

The convenience of central areas such as the Gare du Nord/Gare de l'Est, Pigalle and the eastern districts should be balanced against some less attractive aspects.

Booking a hotel

It is advisable to book in advance (preferably a month or so) all the year round, but especially between Easter and October when more tourists come to Paris.

If you arrive in Paris without having made a reservation, the Office du Tourisme et des Congrès de Paris will be able to help you. They have a hotel reservation service in their main offices, located at *Carrousel du Louvre, 99 rue de Rivoli, tel: 08 92 68 30 00, www.parisinfo.com*, and subsidiary offices at the main stations (except the Gare St-Lazare) as well as at the Tour Eiffel (from May to September only). These act as an emergency service for immediate accommodation. They are closed on Sunday except at the Gare du Nord.

Other accommodation

Self-catering is ideal for those who wish to have complete freedom to sample French cuisine. Self-catering apartments on short-term lets, called *meublés de tourisme*, are available for a minimum of one week and for a maximum of three months.

Below is a selection of agencies and organisations approved by the Office du Tourisme et des Congrès de Paris.

Alcove & Agapes, *8 bis rue Coysevox, 75018. Tel: 01 44 85 06 05; fax: 01 44 85 06 14; www.bedandbreakfastinparis.com. Métro: Guy Moquet.*

Flatotel Expo, *52 rue d'Oradour-sur-Glane, 75015. Tel: 01 45 54 93 45; fax: 01 45 54 93 07.*
Métro: Porte de Versailles.

France-Ermitage, *5 rue Berryer, 75008. Tel: 01 42 56 23 42; fax: 01 42 56 08 99. Métro: Charles-de-Gaulle-Étoile or George V.*

Immovac, *37 avenue de Lowendal, 75015. Tel: 01 45 67 70 00; fax: 01 43 06 12 50; www.immovac.fr. Métro: Cambronne.*

ParisAddress
136 rue Château, 75014. Tel: 01 43 20 91 57; www.parisaddress.com

Another option fast becoming popular is the home exchange, where vacationers agree to swap homes. There are several international home-swap services on the Internet including *www.homelink.org, www.homeexchange.com* and *www.exchangehomes.com*, with listings that can be consulted after becoming a member.

Price for two people in a double room, without breakfast:

£   Under €70
££   €70–150
£££   Over €150

THE HISTORIC CENTRE
Marais
Mije Hostel £
A great option for budget travellers who don't want to compromise on style. These three hostels are all set in the heart of the Marais, in 17th-century former aristocratic residences.
6 rue de Fourcy, 75004. Tel: 01 42 74 23 45. www.mije.com

Hotel Castex ££
A small 3-star hotel located in the fashionable Marais. The rooms are clean and the location perfect.
5 rue Castex, 75004. Tel: 01 42 72 31 52. www.castexhotelparis.com

Marais House £££
This private residence is a fabulous option for travellers who want to experience the city as a local. The exact address is only revealed to those who book.

75003. Tel: 06 16 13 39 90 or 01 42 74 61 36. www.maraishouse.com

Pavillon de la Reine £££
A beautiful oasis of peace and style set in the heart of place des Vosges, this hotel offers 54 individually decorated rooms and suites.
28 place des Vosges, 75003. Tel: 01 40 29 19 19. www. hotelpavillondelareine.com

Saint-Germain-des-Prés
Hotel Jardin de L'Odeon ££
Recently renovated, this 3-star hotel is a great option if you want to stay on the fashionable Rive Gauche without spending a fortune. Some of the rooms even have a private terrace – a real luxury in Paris!
7 rue Casimir Delavigne, 75006. Tel: 01 53 10 28 50. www. hoteljardinodeonparis.com

Hotel Bel-Ami £££
Definitely a hotel with an eye on art and contemporary design, the Bel-Ami also doubles up as a lounge. The rooms are not particularly big, but they are beautiful.

7–11 rue Saint-Benoît, 75006. Tel: 01 42 61 53 53. http://hotel-bel-ami.com

Hotel Pont Royal £££
An institution on the left bank, this hotel has been welcoming celebrities and artists since the 1920s. Among its former guests are Camus, Boris Vian, and painters Miro, Chagall and Buffet.
5–7 rue de Montalembert, 75007. Tel: 01 42 84 70 00. www.hotel-pont-royal.com

NORTH AND WEST OF THE HISTORIC CENTRE
Arc de Triomphe
Four Seasons Hotel: George V £££
Possibly the most lavish hotel in Paris, nestled on one of the main streets off the Champs-Élysées, this building offers 245 guest rooms and suites. Private terraces, 18th-century tapestries and an in-room massage service make this the ultimate in luxury.
31 avenue George V, 75008. Tel: 01 49 52 70 00. www. fourseasons.com/paris

Hotel Crillon £££

Historically the luxury hotel of Paris, with stunning views of the Tour Eiffel and place de la Concorde, the Crillon offers the quintessential 5-star experience.

10 place de la Concorde, 75008. Tel: 01 44 71 15 00. www.crillon.com

Hotel Daniel £££

A small boutique hotel, with a subtle flavour of the East. The decorations are opulent and each room is different. Tucked in a quiet street between the Champs-Élysées and Rue du Faubourg Saint-Honoré, its location is perfect for lovers of shopping and *haute couture*.

8 rue Frédéric Bastiat, 75008. Tel: 01 42 56 17 00. www.hoteldanielparis.com

Hotel Keppler £££

Chic and modern, this small hotel is just a few blocks away from the Champs-Élysées. The staff are very friendly and helpful. It's also one of the few hotels in Paris that allows pets.

12 rue Keppler, 75016. Tel: 01 47 20 65 05. www.keppler.fr

Montmartre
Plug-Inn £

This boutique hostel promises style, comfort and value. Some rooms have bunk beds. A range of facilities including free Internet connection is also available.

7 rue Aristide Bruant, 75018. Tel: 01 42 58 42 58. www.plug-inn.fr

Hôtel Regyn's
Montmartre £–££

Small 2-star hotel with an enviable location in the heart of Montmartre. Rooms are clean and decorated in a cool retro style. Those on the higher floors provide unrestricted views across Paris.

18 place des Abbesses, 75018. Tel: 01 42 54 45 21. www.paris-hotels-montmartre.com

Vintage Hostel £–££

Funky and colourful, this recently opened hostel offers comfortable and clean rooms, each with its own private bathroom, and free Wi-Fi access in the lobby. The perfect choice for travellers coming by train, as it's very close to Gare du Nord station.

73 rue de Dunkerque, 75009. Tel: 01 40 16 16 40. www.vintage-hostel.com

Hotel Particulier
Montmartre £££

Imagine a villa nestled in the heart of Montmartre, in a secret alleyway and surrounded by a perfectly landscaped garden. Welcome to the Hotel Particulier Montmartre. If you manage to secure one of the stunning suites in this hotel, you'll never want to leave Paris.

23 avenue Junot, Pavillon D, 75018. Tel: 01 53 41 81 40. www.hotel-particulier-montmartre

EAST OF THE HISTORIC CENTRE
Mama Shelter ££

Probably one of the most talked about hotels in Paris, Mama Shelter is located in the east, next to Père Lachaise cemetery. Designed by Philippe Starck in a former car park, this hotel has been voted many times as the best business hotel in Paris.

109 rue de Bagnolet, 75020. Tel: 01 43 48 48 48. www.mamashelter.com

Practical guide

Arriving

EU residents visiting France need only show a valid passport to enter the country. This also applies to US citizens, Canadians, Australians and New Zealand nationals, providing the length of their stay does not exceed three months; a visa is required for a longer stay. Visas are obtainable from French embassies and consulates in your own country; apply two months in advance in case of delays.

By air

Paris has two main airports: Charles de Gaulle, 23km (14 miles) northeast of the city, and Orly, 14km (9 miles) south.

Charles de Gaulle (*tel: 01 48 62 22 80, 24 hours a day; www.adp.fr*). Roissyrail, the free airport shuttle bus service, takes passengers to Roissy station where they can board the RER B (train every 8 minutes) for Gare du Nord and Châtelet-les-Halles. Air France (*www.cars-airfrance.com*) buses leave every 12–15 minutes to Porte Maillot, place Charles-de-Gaulle and Gare Montparnasse (from Terminal 2). Regular RATP buses also run from Roissy station to Gare du Nord/Gare de l'Est (No 350), and place de la Nation (No 351). The Roissy bus runs every 15 minutes from Terminal 2 to Opéra.

Orly (*tel: 01 49 75 15 15, 6am– midnight; www.adp.fr*). The new Orlyval fully automatic métro operates a shuttle service (every 10 minutes) between the

airport and the RER B at Antony station, then on to Châtelet-les-Halles. It is more expensive than Orlyrail, which combines the airport bus shuttle service with the RER C to St-Michel-Notre-Dame (every 20 minutes). Air France buses leave every 12 minutes for the Invalides and Gare Montparnasse. Orlybus runs every 15 minutes from the airport to the place Denfert-Rochereau, connecting with the RER B or the métro.

Almost every major national airline carrier in the world flies to Paris, most of them daily, so getting there by air is not a problem. Budget airlines serving Paris from the UK include **easyJet** (*www.easyjet.com*), **bmibaby** (*www.bmibaby.com*), **flybe** (*www.flybe.com*) and **Ryanair** (*www.ryanair.com*), though Ryanair flies to Paris Beauvais Airport, some 70km (43 miles) from the city centre.

By car

If you're happy to take your time getting to Paris and wish to bring your car, you could plump for the good-value option of crossing the channel by ferry. The quickest route is between Dover and Calais, and is served by **P&O** (*Tel: 0871 664 2121. www.poferries.com*) and **SeaFrance** (*Tel: 0871 423 7119. www.seafrance.com*). P&O ferries leave every hour, and the journey takes around an hour and a half. **Brittany Ferries** (*Tel: 0871 244 0744. www.brittany-ferries.co.uk*) run services from Portsmouth, going to the northern towns of Caen, St Malo and Cherbourg. These crossings all take considerably more time. Overnight ferries could, however, be an appealing alternative – particularly if the UK leg of your journey is long.

Whether you arrive by *autoroute* (motorway) or *route nationale* (A road), you will meet the *boulevard* Périphérique, which you can follow until you reach the *porte* (exit) closest to your destination.

Babysitters

Two reliable agencies are: **Babychou** (*31 rue du Moulin de la Pointe, 75013. Tel: 01 43 13 33 23. www.babychou.com*) and **Baby Sitting Services** (*1 place Paul Verlaine, 92100 Boulogne-Billancourt. Tel: 01 46 21 33 16*).

Camping

For information contact the **Fédération Française de Camping et de Caravanning** *78 rue de Rivoli, 75004; tel: 01 42 72 84 08; www.ffcc.fr; métro: Hôtel-de-Ville.*

The following are the most convenient campsites in and around Paris: **Camping du Bois de Boulogne** (*Allée du Bord de l'Eau, 75016; tel: 01 45 24 30 00; métro: Pont-de-Neuilly, then bus No 244*); **Camping International** (*1 rue Johnson, 78600 Maisons-Lafitte; tel: 01 39 12 21 91; 15 minutes from Paris by RER A*); **Camping Campéole** (*Base de Loisirs, 78180, Montigny-le-Bretonneux; tel: 01 30 58 56 20; RER C to St-Quentin-en-Yvelines*); **Camping du Parc de la**

CONVERSION TABLE

FROM	TO	MULTIPLY BY
Inches	Centimetres	2.54
Feet	Metres	0.3048
Yards	Metres	0.9144
Miles	Kilometres	1.6090
Acres	Hectares	0.4047
Gallons	Litres	4.5460
Ounces	Grams	28.35
Pounds	Grams	453.6
Pounds	Kilograms	0.4536
Tons	Tonnes	1.0160

To convert back, for example from centimetres to inches, divide by the number in the third column.

MEN'S SUITS

UK	36	38	40	42	44	46	48
Rest of Europe	46	48	50	52	54	56	58
USA	36	38	40	42	44	46	48

DRESS SIZES

UK	8	10	12	14	16	18
France	36	38	40	42	44	46
Italy	38	40	42	44	46	48
Rest of Europe	34	36	38	40	42	44
USA	6	8	10	12	14	16

MEN'S SHIRTS

UK	14	14.5	15	15.5	16	16.5	17
Rest of Europe	36	37	38	39/40	41	42	43
USA	14	14.5	15	15.5	16	16.5	17

MEN'S SHOES

UK	7	7.5	8.5	9.5	10.5	11
Rest of Europe	41	42	43	44	45	46
USA	8	8.5	9.5	10.5	11.5	12

WOMEN'S SHOES

UK	4.5	5	5.5	6	6.5	7
Rest of Europe	38	38	39	39	40	41
USA	6	6.5	7	7.5	8	8.5

The métro: clearly marked, clean and efficient

Colline (*route de Lagny, 77200 Torcy; tel: 01 60 05 42 32; RER A to Torcy-Marne-la-Vallée, then bus 421*).

Children
Children under four travel free on the Paris transport network if you want to brave the stairs with your pushchair, and under-18s get into national museums free. Baby food and nappies are cheaper in large supermarkets than in pharmacies. Changing tables may be a bit difficult to find, save in the larger department stores.

Climate
Paris enjoys a temperate climate, with moderate rainfall and a good deal of sunshine in spring, summer and even winter. July and August are hottest but also rainiest; January and February are coldest.

Crime
Do not leave anything of value visible in your car. Watch your bag in crowded places. Be particularly careful in areas such as Forum des Halles, Gare du Nord and Gare de l'Est, including the 18th *arrondissement*, and Strasbourg St-Denis. The métro is safe during the day but should be avoided after 11pm.

Driving
Make sure you take your car registration papers and driving licence; an international driving licence is not usually necessary. Your insurance policy covers you for third-party, but if you want comprehensive cover you will need an International Insurance Certificate (green card). In addition, motoring organisations in your own country have accident/breakdown schemes.

If you hire a car, make sure your domestic insurance covers you for

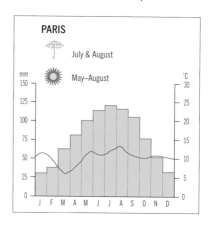

WEATHER CONVERSION CHART
25.4mm = 1 inch
°F = 1.8 × °C + 32

third-party liability; if not, you should obtain top-up cover from your insurers.

Road signs are international. There are four grades of fuel: *gasoil* sometimes spelt *gazolle* (diesel), *super* (98 octane), *sans plomb* (95 octane unleaded) and *super sans plomb* (98 octane unleaded).

A detailed map of Paris that clearly indicates one-way streets is essential. Wearing seat belts is compulsory, and speed is limited to 50kph (31mph) throughout the city, but 80kph (50mph) on the Périphérique.

The *priorité à droite* (giving way to traffic approaching from the right) is strictly observed and bus lanes should be kept clear.

Parking can be a problem and you may decide to leave your car in a long-term car park (ask at your hotel). In the city centre there are parking spaces along the kerb marked *payant* and ticket distributors nearby; the maximum time allowed is two hours (traffic wardens are very efficient). However, parking is free almost everywhere during August. There are also underground car parks at Notre-Dame, Hôtel de Ville, Forum des Halles, Concorde, etc.

All the major international car hire companies are represented in Paris and will arrange for you to pick up a car from various points in the city.
Autorent *Tel: 01 45 54 22 45.*
Avis *Tel: 01 55 38 67 20.*
Europcar *Tel: 01 30 44 93 84.*
Hertz *Tel: 01 47 88 51 51.*

The famous '2-chevaux' car

Electricity
Supply is 220 volts. Two-pin continental plugs are used.

Consulates
Australia *4 rue Jean Rey, 75015. Tel: 01 40 59 33 00.*
Canada *35 avenue Montaigne, 75008. Tel: 01 44 43 29 00. www.amb-canada.fr*
Ireland *4 rue Rude, 75016. Tel: 01 44 17 67 00.*
New Zealand *7 ter rue Léonard de Vinci, 75016. Tel: 01 45 01 43 43.*
South Africa *59 quai d'Orsay, 75007. Tel: 01 53 59 23 23.*
UK *35 rue du Faubourg-St-Honoré, 75008. Tel: 01 44 51 31 00.*
US *2 rue Saint Florentin, 75001. Tel: 01 43 12 22 22.*

Emergency numbers
Police Secours (accidents): *17.*
Pompiers (fire): *18.*

Samu (ambulance): *15 & 01 45 67 50 50.*
SOS Médecins (doctor): *01 47 07 77 77.*
SOS Dentaire (dentist): *01 43 37 51 00*
from 9am to midnight.
Burns *01 44 73 62 54* (children),
01 42 34 17 58 (adults).
Poison Centre *01 40 05 48 48.*
Locksmith *01 47 07 99 99.*

Health

EU residents should obtain a European
Health Insurance Card (available for
UK citizens online at *www.ehic.org.uk*,
from the post office or *tel: 0845 606
2030*) before travelling, to enable them
to receive the same benefits as French
nationals. However, as only 70 to 80
per cent of medical expenses are
reimbursed, even with the card, visitors
are advised to take out separate
medical insurance. Non-EU residents
should obtain the relevant information
from their own country.

National holidays

Offices and banks close on these days,
as do some monuments and museums.
Some shops will remain open. A word
of warning: if a holiday falls on a
Tuesday or Thursday, many places will
automatically close on the Monday or
Friday too. The French like to *faire le
pont*, making a bridge to the weekend
by taking off this extra day.

1 January New Year's Day
Variable Easter Monday
6th Thursday after Easter
Ascension Day

2nd Monday after Ascension Day
Whit Monday
1 May May Day
8 May Victory in Europe Day (1945)
14 July Bastille Day (National Day)
15 August Assumption Day
1 November All Saints' Day
11 November Armistice Day
25 December Christmas Day
Many shops and restaurants are closed
during August.

Lost and found office
Préfecture de Police
36 rue des Morillons, 75015.
Tel: 08 21 00 25 25. Métro: Convention.
Open: Mon–Thur 8.30am–5pm,
Fri 8.30am–4.30pm.

Lost or stolen credit cards
American Express *Tel: 01 47 77 72 00.*
Carte Bleue/VISA *Tel: 08 92 70 57 05*
(costs approx. 0.34 euros/min).
Eurocard/MasterCard
Tel: 01 45 67 84 84.
Diner's Club *Tel: 08 10 31 41 59.*
JCB International *Tel: 01 42 86 06 01.*

Media
Internet
Useful websites about the city include:
www.parisinfo.com
www.cityvox.fr
www.bonjourparis.com
www.paris-anglo.com

Newspapers
There are no evening newspapers in
Paris. *Le Figaro* and *Le Monde* have

supplements or magazines on several days of the week, dealing with cultural events, travelling, books, finance, etc.

There is also a profusion of publications containing the weekly radio and TV programmes, with comments and articles on famous people; *Télérama* is one of the best. The whole range of entertainment offered by the capital is reviewed in detail by two very cheap weekly publications, issued on Wednesday – *Pariscope* and *L'Officiel des Spectacles*. Newspapers and magazines are on sale in kiosks dotted about the city as well as in *Maisons de la Presse* (newsagents), *Journaux-Tabacs* (tobacconists) and some bookshops. Most foreign newspapers are available in the centre, at railway stations and airports.

Radio

Apart from the national stations such as *France Inter* and *France Culture*, there are many local stations that broadcast on FM for the benefit of the Paris region, from *Radio Classique*, the non-stop classical music programme, to *Nostalgie*, a mixture of French songs and light music, and several ethnic stations.

Television

There are six national channels, four public and two private; *Paris Première* is devoted to Paris and its region.

Money matters

The currency in France, as in most of the rest of the EU, is the euro (€). It is divided into 100 cents. There are coins of 1 and 2 euros and of 1, 2, 5, 10, 20 and 50 cents. The notes are of 5, 10, 20, 50, 100, 200 and 500 euros. Exchanging currency is no problem in Paris; it can be done in banks all over the city or in bureaux de change.

Traveller's cheques, if denominated in euros, are accepted as cash in hotels, larger restaurants and stores. You can pay by credit card almost everywhere.

If you need to transfer money quickly, you can use the MoneyGram[SM] Money Transfer service. For more details telephone Freephone *0800 8971 8971* (in the UK).

Opening times

Banks: *Generally Mon–Fri (some banks Tue–Sat) 9am–5pm or 6pm, closed Sunday and holidays.*
Bureaux de change: *6.30am–11pm at airports, 6.30am–10pm at railway stations, 10am–7pm in town.*

If you find yourself short of cash outside these hours, try an ATM. Most now accept foreign credit and debit cards and have easy-to-follow instructions.
Museums: national museums are closed on Tuesday, except the Musée d'Orsay, the Musée Rodin and Versailles, which are closed on Monday. Opening hours are usually 9am–6pm.

Paris museums are generally closed on Monday and free on Sunday (except temporary exhibitions). They are usually open 10am–6pm.

(*Cont. on p184*)

Language

Even if you speak only a little French, the effort will be appreciated. English is widely spoken in tourist areas, less so in the countryside. But whatever your location, you will find that your efforts to speak French, however limited, are appreciated.

yes	oui	**hospital**	hôpital
no	non	**petrol**	essence
please	si'l vous plaît	**airline**	ligne à air
(any request or enquiry should		**Do you speak English?**	Parlez-vous anglais?
be accompanied by this phrase)		**I do not understand**	Je ne comprends pas
thank you	merci	**OK/agreed**	D'accord
good day	bonjour	**Where?**	Où?
good morning		**How much?/**	Combien?
(when addressing anyone in this		**How many?**	
way, it is common courtesy to add		**Excuse me**	Pardon
monsieur for a man, *madame* for a		**Have you a room?**	Avez-vous une chambre?
woman or *mademoiselle* for a girl or		**Have you a room**	Avez-vous une chambre
young woman)		**with a private bath?**	avec bain?
good evening	bonsoir	**How much**	Combien ça coûte?
goodbye	au revoir	**does it cost?**	
yesterday	hier	**I feel ill**	Je suis malade
today	aujourd'hui	**Have you a double**	Avez-vous une chambre à
tomorrow	demain	**room?**	deux lits?
the morning	le matin		
afternoon	l'après-midi		
the evening	le soir		
man	un homme		
woman	une femme		

big	grand	0	zéro	22	vingt-deux
small	petit	1	un, une	30	trente
a lot	beaucoup	2	deux	40	quarante
a little	un peu	3	trois	50	cinquante
open	ouvert	4	quatre	60	soixante
closed	fermé	5	cinq	70	soixante-dix
hot	chaud	6	six	80	quatre-vingts
cold	froid	7	sept	90	quatre-vingt-dix
car	voiture	8	huit	100	cent
railway	gare	9	neuf	200	deux cents
station		10	dix	300	trois cents
bus station	gare routière	11	onze	1,000	mille
bakery	boulangerie	12	douze	2,000	deux mille
supermarket	supermarché	13	treize	1,000,000	un million
bank	banque	14	quatorze		
toilets	toilettes	15	quinze	**Monday**	lundi
post office	PTT, poste	16	seize	**Tuesday**	mardi
stamps	timbres	17	dix-sept	**Wednesday**	mercredi
chemist	pharmacie	18	dix-huit	**Thursday**	jeudi
		19	dix-neuf	**Friday**	vendredi
		20	vingt	**Saturday**	samedi
		21	vingt-et-un	**Sunday**	dimanche

PHRASES

How do you say…(in French)	Comment dites-vous…(en français)
Can you speak slower, please?	Parlez moins vite, s'il vous plaît.
Can you repeat, please?	Pouvez-vous répéter, s'il vous plaît.
Help!	Au secours!
Wait!	Attendez!
Stop!	Arrêtez!
What's that?	Qu'est-ce que c'est?
Can I have..?	je voudrais..
This one/that one	celui-ci/celui-là
It's too expensive	c'est trop cher
I'm just looking	je regarde seulement
What time do you open?	à quelle heure êtes-vous ouverts?
What time do you close?	à quelle heure êtes-vous fermés?
I would like to reserve …	je voudrais réserver…
I have a reservation	j'ai fait une réservation
Single room	chambre pour une personne
Twin room	chambre à lits jumeaux
Double room	chambre pour deux persones/chambre double
With shower	avec douche
With bath	avec bain
Is there a good view?	Est-ce qu'il y a une vue?
Can I see the room?	Est-ce que je peux voir la chambre?
Can I have the key?	Est-ce que je peux avoir la clef?
Is breakfast included?	Est-ce que le petit-déjeuner est compris?
Bed and breakfast	chambres d'hôtes
Can we camp here?	on peut camper ici?
Tent pitch	un emplacement
Youth hostel	auberge de jeunesse
Which way is it to the…château?	Quelle est le chemin pour aller à/au… château?
Where is..?	Où est..?
Is it far?	C'est loin?
Left/right	à gauche/à droite
Straight on	tout droit
Here/there	ici/là
Close/far	près/loin
Corner	coin
Have you got a table?	Avez-vous une table libre?
I want to reserve a table	je voudrais réserver une table
I am a vegetarian	je suis végétarian
I'm having the €20 set menu	je prendrai le menu à vingt euros
The bill please	l'addition s'il vous plaît

Shops: most open weekdays 9am–7pm. Some close noon–2pm, some on Monday morning. Department stores are open daily, except Sunday, from 9.30am–6.30pm, and have a late-closing day midweek. Food shops open at 7am or 8am and close around 8pm; they often close for three hours in the middle of the day. A few also open on Sunday morning.

Organised tours
On foot
The tourism office (*http://en.parisinfo.com*) publishes a book of walks that can be picked up at main museums or information booths. For more scholarly tours, visits and walks **Context Paris** offers a pool of English-speaking experts.
14 Rue Charles V, 75004. Tel: 01 72 81 36 35. www.contexttravel.com

By bicycle
Several bicycle-hire companies organise trips in and around Paris. Contact:
Paris à Velo, c'est Sympa *22 rue Alphonse Baudin, 75011. Tel: 01 48 87 60 01. www.parisvelosympa.com. Métro: Richard Lenoir.*

The latest addition to the Paris transport system is **Vélibe!** – 20,000 bikes across more than 1,000 hop-on and drop-off stations. Anyone with a credit card containing a 'smart chip' can use them. Some also take American Express. The first 30 minutes does not cost extra and you can change bikes as often as you want (*www.velib.fr*).

By bus
Several companies offer tours of the city and excursions to famous places such as Versailles and many others.
Cityrama *4 place des Pyramides, 75001. Tel: 01 44 55 61 00. www.pariscityrama.com. Métro: Palais-Royal.*
Paris Vision *214 rue de Rivoli, 75001. Tel: 01 42 60 30 01. http://fr.parisvision.com. Métro: Tuileries.*
RATP Excursions (run by the Paris Transport Authority); departure from place de la Madeleine; for free brochure and information, *tel: 01 40 06 71 45, www.ratp.info/touristes*. Bookings can be made in advance from place de la Madeleine (*métro: Madeleine*) or from 53 bis quai des Grands Augustins (*métro: St-Michel or Pont Neuf*).

By boat
There are various options for those wanting to take a cruise on the Seine or on the Canal St-Martin.
Bateaux Mouches *Pont de l'Alma, 75007. Tel: 01 45 25 96 10. www.bateaux-mouches.fr. Métro: Pont de l'Alma.*
Bateaux Parisiens *Pont d'Iéna. Tel: 01 44 11 33 44. www.bateauxparisiens.com. Métro: Trocadéro, Bir Hakeim.*
Vedettes du Pont Neuf *Square du Vert-Galant, 75001. Tel: 01 46 33 98 38. www.vedettesdupontneuf.com. Métro: Pont Neuf.*
Canauxrama *13 quai de la Loire, 75019.*

Tel: 01 42 39 15 00.
www.canauxrama.com. Métro: Jaurès.
Paris-Canal 21 quai de la Loire, 75019.
Tel: 01 42 40 96 97. www.pariscanal.com.
Métro: Jaurès.
Vedettes de Paris Port de Suffren,
75007. Tel: 01 44 18 19 50.
www.vedettesdeparis.com

Helicopter tours
Exclusive Tours 8 rue du Faubourg
Poissonière, 75010. Tel: 01 42 33 12 51.
www.exclusive-tours.com.
Métro: Bonne Nouvelle.

Pharmacies
The following remain open outside
normal hours:
British and American Pharmacy
1 rue Auber, 75009.
Tel: 01 42 65 88 29. Open: daily except
Sunday until 8pm. Métro: Opéra.
Pharmacie Anglaise
62 Champs-Élysées, 75008. Tel: 01 43
59 22 52. Open: daily noon–10pm.
Métro: Franklin-Roosevelt.
Pharma Presto
Pharma Presto operates a 24-hour
delivery service (livraison).
Tel: 01 42 42 42 50.

Places of worship
St Michael's Anglican Church 5 rue
d'Aguesseau, 75008. Tel: 01 47 42 70 88.
Métro: Madeleine.
St Joseph's Catholic Church
50 avenue Hoche, 75008.
Tel: 01 42 27 28 56.
Métro: Charles-de-Gaulle-Étoile.

Church of Scotland 17 rue Bayard,
75008. Tel: 01 48 78 47 94.
Métro: Franklin-Roosevelt.
Synagogue La Victoire 44 rue de la
Victoire, 75009. Tel: 01 40 82 26 26.
Métro: Notre-Dame-de-Lorette.
Grande Mosquée 39 rue Geoffroy-St-
Hilaire, 75005. Tel: 01 45 35 97 33.
Métro: Jussieu or Place Monge.

Police
The **Préfecture de Police** (7 boulevard
du Palais, 75004; tel: 01 58 80 80 80) on
Île de la Cité is the police headquarters.
There are commissariats de police
(police stations) in each arrondissement.
In case of emergency, tel: 17.

Post offices
Bureaux de poste are open Mon–Fri
8am–7pm, Sat 8am–noon.
  The main office (52 rue du Louvre,
75001; tel: 01 40 28 20 00; métro:
Louvre-Rivoli) is open 24 hours a day,
7 days a week. The address for poste
restante mail is: Poste Restante, 52 rue
du Louvre, 75001 Paris RP, France.
Stamps can also be bought in a tabac
(tobacconist). Postboxes are yellow,
free-standing, or set into a wall.

Public transport
The métro/RER/suburban
railway/buses network is run jointly by
the Régie Autonome des Transports
Parisiens (RATP) and the Société
Nationale des Chemins de Fer (SNCF).
For general information, telephone:
(Cont. on p188)

Practical guide

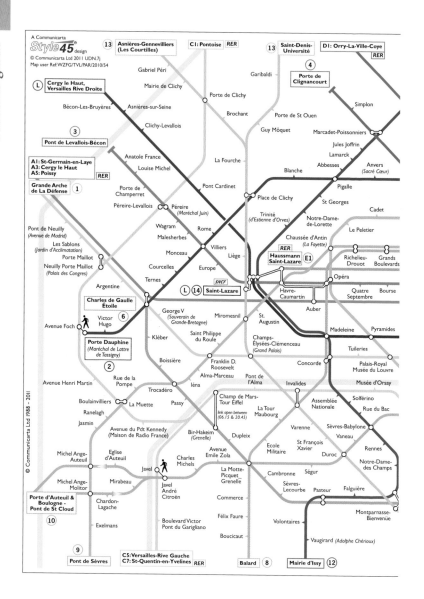

A Communicarta
Style45 design
© Communicarta Ltd 2011 UDN.7)
Map user Ref:WZFG/TVL/PAR/2010/54

13 Asnières-Gennevilliers (Les Courtilles)

C1: Pontoise RER

13 Saint-Denis-Université

D1: Orry-La-Ville-Coye RER

Gabriel Péri

Garibaldi

4

Porte de Clignancourt

L Cergy le Haut, Versailles Rive Droite

Mairie de Clichy

Porte de Clichy

Simplon

Bécon-Les-Bruyères

Asnières-sur-Seine

Brochant

Porte de St Ouen

3

Clichy-Levallois

Guy Môquet

Marcadet-Poissonniers

Pont de Levallois-Bécon

Jules Joffrin

Lamarck

A1: St-Germain-en-Laye
A3: Cergy le Haut
A5: Poissy RER

Anatole France

La Fourche

Abbesses

Anvers (Sacré Cœur)

Louise Michel

Blanche

Grande Arche de La Défense **1**

Porte de Champerret

Pont Cardinet

Pigalle

Péreire (Maréchal Juin)

St Georges

Cadet

Péreire-Levallois

Place de Clichy

Notre-Dame-de-Lorette

Pont de Neuilly (Avenue de Madrid)

Wagram

Rome

Trinité (d'Estienne d'Orves)

Le Peletier

Les Sablons (Jardin d'Acclimatation)

Maleherbes

Chaussée d'Antin (La Fayette)

Porte Maillot

Monceau

Villiers

Liège

RER

Richelieu-Drouot

Grands Boulevards

Neuilly Porte Maillot (Palais des Congres)

Courcelles

Europe

Haussmann Saint-Lazare **E1**

Argentine

Ternes

SNCF

Opéra

Charles de Gaulle Étoile

L **14** **Saint-Lazare**

Havre-Caumartin

Quatre Septembre

Bourse

Victor Hugo **6**

George V (Souverain de Grande-Bretagne)

Miromesnil

St. Augustin

Auber

Avenue Foch

Kléber

Saint Philippe du Roule

Champs-Élysées-Clémenceau (Grand Palais)

Madeleine

Pyramides

Porte Dauphine (Maréchal de Lattre de Tassigny)

2

Boissière

Franklin D. Roosevelt

Concorde

Tuileries

Avenue Henri Martin

Rue de la Pompe

Iéna

Alma-Marceau

Pont de l'Alma

Invalides

Palais-Royal Musée du Louvre

Trocadéro

Musée d'Orsay

Boulainvilliers

La Muette

Passy

Champ de Mars-Tour Eiffel

Assemblée Nationale

Solférino

Ranelagh

link open between (06.15 & 20.45)

La Tour Maubourg

Rue du Bac

Jasmin

Avenue du Pdt Kennedy (Maison de Radio France)

Bir-Hakeim (Grenelle)

Duplex

Varenne

Sèvres-Babylone

Vaneau

Michel Ange-Auteuil

Eglise d'Auteuil

Javel

Charles Michels

Avenue Emile Zola

Ecole Militaire

St François Xavier

Duroc

Rennes

Michel Ange-Molitor

Mirabeau

Javel André Citroën

La Motte-Picquet-Grenelle

Cambronne

Ségur

Notre-Dame-des Champs

Porte d'Auteuil & Boulogne - Pont de St Cloud

Chardon-Lagache

Commerce

Sèvres-Lecourbe

Pasteur

Falguière

10

Félix Faure

Volontaires

Montparnasse-Bienvenüe

Exelmans

Boulevard Victor Pont du Garigliano

Boucicaut

Vaugirard (Adolphe Chérioux)

9

Pont de Sèvres

C5: Versailles-Rive Gauche
C7: St-Quentin-en-Yvelines RER

Balard **8**

Mairie d'Issy **12**

© Communicarta Ltd 1988 - 2011

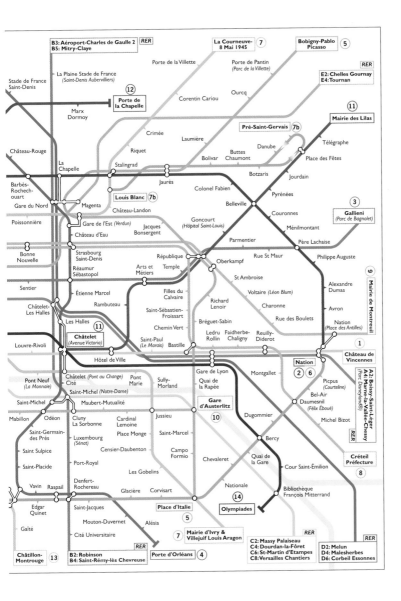

RATP *Tel: 08 92 68 77 14; www.ratp.fr.* English-speaking service, *tel: 08 92 68 41 14.*
SNCF *Tel: 08 36 35 35 35* (6am–10pm). Passes, available from the main tourist office, métro, RER and railway stations, entitle visitors to use the whole network for one, two, three or five days.

By Eurostar
Travelling by Eurostar may be the best way to reach Paris. With trains leaving every hour, and more frequently during rush hours, tickets can be much cheaper than travelling by plane or by car if booked far in advance.

Most Eurostar trains have a direct non-stop service from St Pancras International to Gare du Nord, but some will also stop at Ashford International and Ebbsfleet International.

The train journey is just over two hours; Standard, Standard Premier and Business Premier class tickets are available on all trains. *www.eurostar.com*

Paris's six main-line railway stations are within easy reach of the city centre:
Gare d'Austerlitz *55 quai d'Austerlitz, 75013; RER C and métro line 10.*
Gare de l'Est *place du 11 novembre 1918, 75010; métro lines 4 and 7.*
Gare de Lyon *20 boulevard Diderot, 75012; RER A and métro line 1.*
Gare Montparnasse *17 boulevard de Vaugirard 75015; métro lines 4, 12 and 13.*
Gare du Nord *18 rue de Dunkerque, 75010; RER B and D and métro line 4.*
Gare St-Lazare *13 rue d'Amsterdam, 75008; RER E and métro line 14.*

Day and night charges are indicated inside taxi cabs; a supplement is due if you board a taxi at a railway station or airport, or have more than one suitcase.

For complaints contact: **Service Taxis, Préfecture de Police**, *36 rue des Morillons, 75015 Paris. Tel: 08 21 00 25 25.*

Sport   *See pp158–61.*
Allo-Sports (*tel: 01 42 76 54 54; 10.30am–5pm except weekends*) gives information on sports events and clubs.

Student accommodation
Call **Fédération Unie des Auberges de Jeunesse** for information (*tel: 01 44 89 87 27; fax: 01 44 89 87 49; www.fuaj.org*). Several youth associations offer cheap lodging:
CROUS *39 avenue Georges-Bernanos, 75005. Tel: 01 40 51 55 55; www.crous-paris.fr*
Ligue Française des Auberges de Jeunesse Booking systems: *67 rue Vergniaud, 75013. Tel: 01 44 16 78 78. www.auberges-de-jeunesse.com*

Sustainable tourism
Thomas Cook is a strong advocate of ethical and fairly traded tourism and believes that the travel experience should be as good for the places visited as it is for the people who visit them. That's why we firmly support The Travel Foundation, a charity that develops solutions to help improve and protect holiday destinations, their environment, traditions and culture. To find out

what you can do to make a positive difference to the places you travel to and the people who live there, please visit *www.makeholidaysgreener.org.uk*

Telephones

Calls from hotels are more expensive than from a post office or a telephone booth. Some of these are still coin-operated, but the majority work on a *télécarte* (phonecard) available in post offices and tobacconists.

Numbers in France comprise ten digits. All numbers for Paris and its outskirts begin *01*. There are no area codes. For the operator dial *13*; for directory enquiries dial *12*.

To make an international call, dial *00* then the country code (Australia *61*, New Zealand *64*, UK *44*, US and Canada *1*), then the area code (minus any initial *0*) followed by the number.

Time

GMT plus 1 hour (winter), plus 2 hours (summer).

Tipping

Service is included on bills in cafés and restaurants but you might want to leave a tip as well. It is also customary to tip hotel porters and chambermaids, museum guides, usherettes in cinemas and taxi drivers.

Toilets

There are public toilets in department stores, cafés and restaurants, and coin-operated booths on the pavements.

Tourist offices

Office du Tourisme et des Congrès de Paris *Carrousel du Louvre, 99 rue de Rivoli, 75001 (tel: 08 92 68 30 00; open: daily 10am–6pm; métro: George V).* There are also branches at all the railway stations, and at the Eiffel Tower. The **Mairie de Paris** has a Bureau d'Accueil at *29 rue de Rivoli, 75004 (tel: 01 42 76 43 43; open: daily 9am–6pm; closed: Sunday; métro: Hôtel de Ville).*

Travellers with disabilities

Ease of access to sights, museums, theatres and other public places in Paris is improving as the city makes a real effort to welcome visitors with disabilities.

Several brochures on various aspects of daily life are available by mail order directly from local organisations such as: Association des Paralysés de France, Délégation de Paris, *17 boulevard Auguste Blanqui, 75013 (tel: 01 40 78 69 00),* and CTNERHI (Centre Technique National d'Études et de Recherche sur les Handicaps et Inadaptations), *236 bis rue de Tolbiac, 75013 (tel: 01 45 65 59 00, www.ctnerhi.com.fr).*

Access in Paris, a fully researched guide for wheelchair users and walkers with disabilities, is available free from Access Projects, *39 Bradley Gardens, London W13 8HE, www.accessinparis.org.* It deals with all aspects of travelling to Paris, and how to make the most of it once you are there.

Practical guide

Index

Acknowledgements

Thomas Cook Publishing wishes to thank the photographers, picture libraries and other organisations, to whom copyright belongs, for the photographs in this book.

AA PHOTO LIBRARY P Enticknap 68, 85; P Kenwood 80; D Noble 126, 127, 128, 131, 134, 136, 138; A Souter 31, 44, 55, 89, 94, 103, 113, 115, 122, 153, 167; and the remaining by K Patterson
DREAMSTIME.COM Lwilk 1, King-tut 41, Dimenty 53, Arenysam 58, Jkelcher 59, G Bond 60, Taolmor 76, Abadesign 79, Jaspe 104, Solena432 139, D Talsan 165
DAVID HENRY 35, 38, 112
ISTOCKPHOTO michele lugaresi 19, Lambert (Bart) Parren, 25
PETULIA MELIDEO 5, 109, 152
PICTURE COLOUR LIBRARY 45
JONATHAN SMITH 9, 11, 13, 24, 27, 28, 39, 48, 54, 70, 72, 81, 88, 98, 99, 108, 119, 121, 133, 149, 151, 154, 163
SPECTRUM COLOUR LIBRARY 140
THOMAS COOK 50, 164
WORLD PICTURES 17, 34, 123

For CAMBRIDGE PUBLISHING MANAGEMENT LIMITED:
Project editor: Kate Taylor
Typesetter: Trevor Double
Proofreaders: Emily Anderson & Jan McCann
Indexer: Marie Lorimer

SEND YOUR THOUGHTS TO
BOOKS@THOMASCOOK.COM

We're committed to providing the very best up-to-date information in our travel guides and constantly strive to make them as useful as they can be. You can help us to improve future editions by letting us have your feedback. If you've made a wonderful discovery on your travels that we don't already feature, if you'd like to inform us about recent changes to anything that we do include, or if you simply want to let us know your thoughts about this guidebook and how we can make it even better – we'd love to hear from you.

Send us ideas, discoveries and recommendations today and then look out for your valuable input in the next edition of this title.

Emails to the above address, or letters to the traveller guides Series Editor, Thomas Cook Publishing, PO Box 227, Coningsby Road, Peterborough PE3 8SB, UK.

Please don't forget to let us know which title your feedback refers to!